A Matter of Chastity

John and Ella Dwyer pose for a wedding photo. The two married November 28, 1898, in Chicago. By then calling herself Ella instead of Ellen, the bride looks somber in her long wedding dress. John Dwyer, born in 1872 in County Clare, Ireland, came to Chicago about 1890. He met Ella after she left western Kansas following her trial. They traveled to New Almelo, Kansas, with plans to marry, but the local priest would not perform the ceremony. They found a priest in Chicago who united them in matrimony. By November 1899 they lived in a sod house in Graham County, Kansas, and expected their first child. (Photo courtesy of Caryl Finnerty.)

A Matter of Chastity

of

Chastity

The High Plains Saga
of a Woman's Revenge

by
Douglas Yocom

DUSTY COVER BOOKS
Portland, Oregon
2005

Published in the United States by
DUSTY COVER BOOKS
4 S. E. 84th Avenue
Portland, Oregon 97216
Dustycvr@teleport.com
(503) 254-5146

ISBN 0-9771177-0-7

Library of Congress Cataloging-in-Publication Data
Yocom, Douglas.
A matter of chastity : the saga of a woman's revenge / by
Douglas
Yocom. — 1st ed.
    p. cm.
Includes bibliographical references.
ISBN 0-9771177-0-7 (hardcover : alk. paper)
    1. Lunney, Ellen Catherine, 1876?–1957—Trials, litigation, etc.
2. Trials (Murder)—Kansas—Norton County. 3. Trials (Rape)
—Kansas--Norton County. 4. Frontier and pioneer life—Kansas
—Sources.   I. Title.
KF223.L885Y63 2005
364.152'3'09781155--dc22

                              2005020278

Produced under the direction of
THE ARTHUR H. CLARK CO.
P.O. Box 14707
Spokane, WA 99214

FOR ELLA
who endured more than we knew

Illustrations

THE LUNNEY FAMILY, EARLY 1890S
The Lunneys pose in a buggy pulled by two large black horses. Ellen, in white, is seated at the rear with a bonnet. Tom, standing, is the taller child. The Lunneys later would say the buggy was a common old lumber wagon, but others said it was a fashionable spring wagon – which it was. (Photo courtesy of Caryl Finnerty.)

One

Tuesday, July 31, 1894

If John Lunney could have driven slower, he would have.

The wagon rattled along the dusty road that ran beside a pasture, its once-beautiful face pockmarked by the hollows of hundreds of prairie dogs. They scurried from hole to hole, ever watchful for a youngster like Will Lunney with a rifle who could pick them off one by one or cause them to scamper down into their burrows. That may have been how Ellen Lunney felt, wishing she could hide forever in one of the hundreds of prairie dog holes.

Ellen was crowded, jammed between her parents in the front seat of the buggy. Pulled by two large and matched black horses, the Lunney's spring wagon, or buggy – later there would be debate as to whether it really was a fashionable carriage or an old farm wagon – moved slowly over the rutted road. On one side of Ellen sat her father, John Lunney, who kept his hands tightly on the reins. He wore his heavy Sunday suit and said little as he guided the horses along the country road that had grown only wide enough for two wagons to pass. Ellen's mother Anna sat on the other side of Ellen. An attractive woman at age forty-one, Anna was almost twenty years younger than her husband. She kept up a soft, comforting conversation with her daughter, hoping to relieve the tension of the trip. She recognized that Ellen felt captured by forces she did not control. Ellen sat rigidly, answering her mother in short sentences.

For Ellen, the trip was suffocating. More than anything she wanted relief. An end to the hell of the last week. Death? That would be better than living, considering how she felt about herself.

The three well-dressed buggy travelers approached their destination, the Thuma farm. Two Lunney sons, Tom and Will, lagged but were not far behind. Tom rode in a wagon with John McKeniff, who was John Lunney's nephew but treated by the Lunney family as if he were a son.

The western Kansas plains had begun warming in the July sun although it was not yet eight o'clock in the morning. Ellen, wearing a long cape, or cloak, and sitting close to her parents, felt the day's heat warming her thin body.

John Lunney had been confused about where he should go, the Thuma School or the Thuma farm. The wagon neared the large farm of Squire D. H. Thuma. The school lay beyond. First, he would stop there, at the Thuma farm.

But soon all three persons in the wagon saw that some of the McEnroe family had arrived. John saw from the look on his daughter's face that she did not want to go into the Thuma home. Not now.

He understood. John left his wife and daughter in the wagon and went alone into Thuma's. He didn't stay long. Soon he returned to the wagon and said they needed to go on to the Thuma School, the whitewashed, one-room structure that had been built nearby to teach the children of the farmers how to read and write and do their arithmetic. Grades one to eight, if the kids could stick it out that long.

James McEnroe and two sons left the Thuma house about the same time. The McEnroes did not have such a fancy carriage as the Lunneys. The father and sons were on horseback and would be at the school before the Lunneys. John Lunney toyed with the halter of the horses, wasting minutes so they would not be too close to the McEnroes. Better to keep some distance.

After the McEnroes left – Gene was not with them – John Lunney climbed back into the buggy and drove the horses slowly toward the Thuma School.

This time John Lunney walked the team to the school. He traveled so slowly that John McKeniff passed the Lunneys in a wagon.

10

McKeniff had left the Lunney house more than a half hour after the Lunneys. Now McKeniff had two passengers: Willie Lunney, and he had picked up Squire Thuma. Tom, the oldest Lunney son, passed on horseback. Tom had started the trip in the wagon with McKeniff, and Willie had begun the trip on horseback. They swapped at Thuma's place.

The schoolyard had nearly filled with horses and wagons when John Lunney arrived. He found a fence post where he could tie the team. But first he helped Anna and his daughter Ellen out of the wagon. Will appeared and began helping his father tend the horses.

Anna and Ellen walked toward the school house door, the south entrance. They looked inside. Forty to fifty persons sat on school benches awaiting the county attorney who would handle the arraignment and preliminary hearing. Anna and Ellen expressed their surprise at the size of the crowd so early in the day. Most of the seats had been taken. The room quickly grew silent. Anna took Ellen's arm. She led her daughter forward.

All eyes focused on Ellen, young and attractive in her cape and summer dress. Despite the crowd, her eyes fell on Gene McEnroe. He was seated in the next-to-back row talking to someone. Gene turned. Their eyes met. Gene gave Ellen a big smile. Or was it a leer?

Ellen knew the meaning of that leer. She left her mother's side and walked over behind Gene McEnroe. Ellen reached inside her cape.

Everyone in the room stopped talking. Except for the sounds of horses outside the school, the room fell quiet.

Ellen pulled out a revolver, a long six-shooter almost too large for a small lady. She aimed it at Gene.

A little lady with a big gun. And nobody in the room knew what she was going to do with it.

Two

Ellen Lunney developed a reputation as a quiet, deeply religious girl, not unusual for someone growing up in the isolation of the rural, desolate high plains. The plains did that to you. Except for Sunday trips to church, Ellen could go for days without seeing anyone except her parents, her brothers and sisters or a neighbor or two who dropped by. Neighbors shared what they had, and their coming and going often resulted from a need to borrow or return a tool or a household item. Or maybe it was the need for conversation, to see another human being. The Kansas plains could be so lonely that the desolation drove many to madness.

Early in her life, the solitude of the prairie seems to have crept into the veins of young Ellen. Those who visited the Lunney farm would remark about how quiet Ellen could be. To those meeting her for the first time, she seemed to shrink into the background and let her parents be the ones to extend the greetings. Often she suddenly appeared carrying fresh bread and preserves for the visitors. But Ellen seldom volunteered information. She responded to questions, and it was only then the visitor realized that here was a young lady at a major decision point in her life. Ellen had qualified as a school teacher, one of the few professional positions a women could hold in the 1890s. Or she could become a farm wife, a raiser of children, a keeper of the household and a comforter to her husband. The daughter of homesteaders, she seemed destined one moment to develop into a strong, farm-bred wife; the next moment she appeared almost frail, maybe too fragile to manage a farm family and home, something that confounded some observers. She favored her profile, knowing that she seemed more attractive when she didn't look straight at you. Her profile also showed attractive curves had developed, and they appeared through the homemade print dresses she wore around the house in summer. She was straight backed, fair skinned and medium height. Her face had a softness strengthened by a firm, straight jaw. Her brown hair and light complexion was typical of a young Irish girl. She wore her hair pulled back, sometimes in a braid, which emphasized her beauty. She was attractive but not beautiful. She carried no extra weight as she learned early to expend her energy working around the farm. Ellen wanted to be liked. Neighbors later would say that Ellen was obedient to her parents, polite to everyone and concerned about the welfare of others. A model child. Not the type to get into trouble.

Ellen Catherine Lunney was born on a farm homesteaded by her father a few miles southwest of Lenora, Kansas, located in Norton County, which is jammed against the Nebraska border. Go three counties to the west and one bumps into the state of Colorado.

One looking for the Old West would have found it here. Until the 1870s, the rolling hills and flat prairie overflowed with buffalo, which fed and sustained a nomadic nation of American Indians. Then the forced removal of thousands of Indians began. Railroad men, squatters and land speculators pushed the federal government into manipulating Indian treaties to ensure tribal destruction and the killing of millions of buffalo. Soon the barriers to settlement disappeared, and the race for open land on the Kansas frontier began.

Present-day, twenty-first-century Americans may not understand how marginal life could be along the frontier. People died daily from gunshot wounds, rattlesnake bites, Indian arrows, starvation and vigilante hangings. These nineteenth century seekers of land and homes greatly feared the unpredictable Indians and the potential of Indian attacks, and they felt they had good reason to feel that way. The federal government did not provide much protection for the pioneers until the railroads began laying track into the area in 1872.

The law along the frontier went through a comprehensive transformation from what was imposed by federal marshals or locally hired lawmen. Local Kansas histories of this period are filled with short news items about someone being shot or hanged for "suspicion" of some crime, often thievery of a horse. Disputes were settled by whomever had the most pistols and rifles, not who was right or wrong. Stories abound about those along the wild frontier who were killed for minor reasons, particularly if whiskey were involved. Vigilante enforcement of a code of behavior disappeared slowly. By the 1890s circuit-riding judges somewhat educated in the law meted out a stern but more measured justice.

Ellen's father, John Lunney, ventured onto the wild, treacherous prairie and homesteaded in 1873. A year after coming to Kansas, John Lunney, at age thirty-eight, picked a partner much like he had selected his prime bottom land. He fell for an attractive girl, one of the Dunlap daughters. Anna Dunlap was nineteen, and the two married and set about what others on the frontier did, scratching out a living while producing a brood of children.

Into such a land did John and Anna Lunney bring Ellen Catherine. The Lunneys did not remain long in the sod house they constructed along Marsh Creek, choosing better land four miles to the north along the Solomon River, which would become the Lunney's permanent home and where six more children would be born. They left the soddie for a new farm and frame house that lay halfway between the small towns of Lenora and New Almelo, seven miles apart. Here, along the north fork of the Solomon River, their homesteader neighbors included several families of Irish immigrants, including Anna's parents, the Dunlaps.

The Gabriel Dunlap and James Gilleece families had fled Ireland's frequent famines and settled near Renfrew, Ontario, Canada. It was easier in the mid-nineteenth century to cross the Atlantic and immigrate to Canada than to enter the United States. But by 1873, the Dunlaps and Gilleeces looked to the south and traveled together to homestead in western Kansas.

The Dunlaps and Gilleeces scurried across the border separating

Canada and the United States. No one guarded the border in those days. The Dunlaps must have considered their escape complete from the cruelties of the nineteenth century Irish economy when they reached the North American continent. The 1900 U. S. Census indicated that Anna Dunlap Lunney hadn't bothered to become a naturalized citizen in her new county.

The four Dunlap boys developed into excellent horsemen. Many wild horses roamed the prairies. Mature wild horses could not be domesticated as easily as young colts and fillies. The Dunlap boys would ride out in the winter after a big snow and drive the colts into deeper snow, rope them, hobble them by tying their feet together and leave them until the next day. Then they loaded them on sleds and brought them home, where they were turned loose in a sod and pole corral. They trained the horses for two years before selling them.

The Lunneys, Dunlaps and Gilleeces considered themselves part of the community of New Almelo, a tiny outpost in the southwestern corner of Norton County, Kansas. At first the village was known as the "French Settlement." But Canadian Catholics and Germans began arriving and homesteaded along the Solomon River, and Catholics of German and Irish descent soon dominated.

The first community center of the homesteaders was a sod stockade, or fort, called New Elm, large enough to take in teams and wagons during Indian scares. Later a town site called "Almelo," named after a community in The Netherlands, was laid out around the fort. But by the 1880s the hopes of the community had faded because of a lack of a railroad connection. New Almelo never grew much beyond the size it achieved by 1882, and it never surpassed being a hamlet with a Catholic church and a school as its main anchors.

The residents also considered themselves part of the community where they spent much of their money: a market town that lay nearest their home – Lenora, Clayton, Selden or Allison. New Almelo never achieved sufficient size to serve the farming community, and for the Lunneys and those living nearby that role fell to

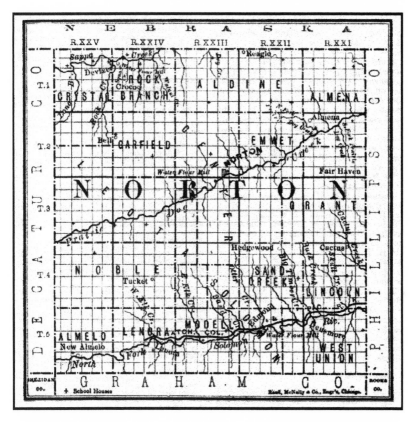

Norton County, located in northwest Kansas, is bordered by Nebraska on the north. Three counties lie between it and the Colorado border. The Lunney and McEnroe families lived along the North Fork of the Solomon River, at the lower edge of the map, between New Almelo and Lenora. Norton, the county seat, is on Prairie Dog Creek, more than twenty miles from the scene of the rape and murder. Map circa 1883.

the town a few miles to the east, Lenora, with its railroad connection. The town was named after Lenora Harrison, the only white woman living on the Solomon River west of Kirwin in the winter of 1872. Supposedly a woman of unusual beauty, Lenora's name was selected for the new town site by rough men who had not seen another woman in some time.

17

Dewain Delp, an early attorney in Lenora, described the character of early residents:

> There were only a few people living in Norton County, probably around 200 in 1872. Ninety nine percent of these were men – a rough and motley crew they were, not the 'noble pioneer' that historians have glorified, but men of the world, adventurers, opportunists, and even thieves – hard, rough and cunning. They were for the most part men who had not been too successful in the home community back east, so had moved on further west with the philosophy that 'the early bird gets the worm' and the worms are 'easy picking.' Some were trappers and hunters, others traders along the line of a huckster, who carried his stock of goods in his wagon – salt pork, flour, salt, whiskey, gun powder, shot, perhaps guns and a few clothes. Then there were the 'horse traders' and 'land scalpers'– men hoping to sell land to the real homesteaders whom they knew would soon be arriving.

~

Soon after they arrived along the Solomon River, the Irish began intermarrying. James Gilleece married Mary Dunlap, Anna's sister, a union that produced a family of four daughters and two sons, Margaret, Katie, Mary, Sadie, John and William. John Hickert, who grew up in the community, relates how real was the threat of Indians.

> In 1876 the Pawnee Indians were hunting, fishing and trapping along the creeks. They were a friendly tribe and frequently visited the settlers' homes. One day an Indian woman and her little baby visited Mary Gilleece. William, Mrs. Gilleece's little baby, was in his cradle. The Indian woman took a great fancy to William and immediately wanted to trade her little girl for the little white boy. Fortunately for Mrs. Gilleece, Mary Knutson happened to be visiting her that day. Between the two ladies they finally persuaded the Indian woman to compromise when Mrs. Gilleece gave the little girl a bright red dress trimmed with blue buttons, and an all-wool shawl.

Indians in the area generally seemed friendly, but the settlers always saw them as threatening. Ellen Lunney told her children and grandchildren a story of how her mother had hidden her in a wooden box when Indians visited her home. Anna Lunney did not want the Indians to see the little girl. The Lunneys, Dunlaps and Gilleeces had reason to be wary as the Indian threat did not dissipate until after 1878, when a band of Cheyennes trekking to their lands in the Dakota Black Hills massacred forty settlers in neighboring Decatur County.

Mary Dunlap Gilleece survived the Indians but perished from another threat, a rampaging prairie fire. It trapped Mary and her twelve-year-old daughter Margaret, who were trying to rescue livestock from the searing flames. They fled to a ravine but died two days later from burns suffered in the fire. They are buried in New Almelo Cemetery. A memorial monument in the cemetery marks their tragic deaths.

~

Homesteaders like the Lunneys who lived found a rough life. They loved, married, delivered children and died, often without leaving the area where they created their first homesite. In 1877 and 1878, a second wave of settlers flooded into the area, most of them arriving from other midwestern states. The James McEnroe family came from nearby Graham County. The best bottom land already had been taken years earlier by families such as the Lunneys and Dunlaps. The best upland, too, had been settled. Virgil Dieterich, writing "Lenora's Heritage" in the informative booklet, "A History of Lenora, Kansas," quotes an item saying that before 1879 "Lenora's population was exceedingly small and her businesses very few indeed." But the "boom of 1879" brought a group of new businesses and construction of much of the downtown of Lenora. By 1879, or within two or three years, the following businesses existed: Commercial House hotel, a boarding house, a lunch room, a general merchandise store, a meat market, a drug store, a furniture store, a hardware, a seller of boots and shoes, a grocery, a watchmaker, a flour miller that did custom work, a barber shop, a billiards parlor supposedly "one of the most orderly halls in the state," a blacksmith, a lumber company, two justices of the peace, a notary, a retired lawyer "prepared to give advice whenever he can not avoid it," a livery, a land agency in "the general land business," a post office, two doctors, a newspaper although a second sometimes was printed, and a railroad. The first paper, the *Lenora Leader*, was a

Early Lenora, looking south toward the Solomon River (trees). The downtown is beyond the trees. The photograph probably was taken in the 1890s. (Photo courtesy of Kansas State Historical Society, Topeka.)

Greenback paper supporting currency reform for the debtor farmers, but it became Republican after a change of ownership. A dentist visited Lenora on Mondays. The Central Branch of the Missouri Pacific Railroad provided passenger and freight service from the east. The line from eastern Kansas was extended to Lenora in 1881, where it terminated. By 1883 horse-drawn stages took passengers to Oberlin, Sheridan, Norton and WaKeeney. The Norton stage left Lenora daily at 7 a.m and arrived at 11 a.m. It left Norton at 2 p.m. and arrived back in Lenora at 6 p.m.

". . . we (Lenora) still are in need of a harness shop, photograph gallery, millinery and dress-making establishment and a good creamery," said the summary written by W. C. Thornton in March 1882. The First State Bank was formed in 1884, two years after the first newspaper, the Lenora Leader, began publication.

Early businessmen built stores from wood, but bricks became

fashionable and practical when the railroad arrived. Almost on the same train came the artisans and stonemasons capable of building stronger structures one or two stories tall.

~

Late in 1874 Joseph F. Glidden received a patent for barbed wire and literally changed the American western landscape in a few short years. More than anyone, Glidden killed the American cowboy. He was replaced by the farmer on the rugged, isolated frontier of western Kansas as it transformed itself into a fenced, cultivated land with rough dirt roads or trails connecting farms to market towns. Many youngsters riding their horses across the unbroken sod pastures probably still thought of themselves as young cowboys, not dirt farmers, but the truth was that the land never would return to the wild days of the gunfighters shooting it out in the streets while the good citizens of the village huddled and hid in their homes. Young men might still carry rifles or revolvers, but they used them to shoot the troublesome prairie dogs or more edible game. The land had been altered forever into farms served by railroads and looking to a national market to their sell wheat, cattle and other commodities. The introduction of the refrigerator car meant that beef could be shipped longer distances after the cattle from the West reached stockyards in Kansas City, Omaha or Chicago.

Nothing had as much effect as wire fences in stopping the free movement on the range and channeling horses and wagons onto rough country roads. Newly settled farmers had learned to fence their property with hedgerows or stones. Then barbed wire quickly changed the western landscape and how buffalo, Indians and anyone else traveled across the countryside. Fence posts and barbed wire could be shipped west by rail. Farmers soon began fencing land that they were homesteading but on which they often did not have title. Roads that formerly meandered across the prairie pasture began following fencerows, hedgerows and section lines.

Kansas' population surpassed 360,000 in 1870, climbed to almost a million by 1880 and surged to 1,420,000 in 1890. The western part of the state was settled in those two decades. In that time the cowboy, the Indian and the buffalo were swept away by cultural currents that left lasting imprints on the high plains.

Western Kansas' population grew diverse, partly because town promoters advertised in European newspapers, and land-hungry people from Russia, Germany, Bohemia, Czechoslovakia, France and the low countries came by the thousands. New Almelo, originally called the French Settlement, attracted Catholics from western Europe in the 1880s, and most were neither French nor Irish but more likely Bohemians, Czechs or Russians. Some of the west's new arrivals clustered in groups and built whole towns. Historians called them "colonists" because they brought their culture and language and came in organized groups. As in New Almelo, Catholics built magnificent cathedrals in towns such as Catherine, Walker, Munjor, Liebenthal, Pfeifer, Ellis, Victoria and Schoenchen, their spires ascending high into the heavens above the furrowed plains.

$\sim$

By 1894 an estimated 1,000 persons lived in Norton, county seat of Norton County, Kansas. The town had built a court house that served as a permanent, locked building for keeping the county records from being looted by a faster-growing, competing city that knew what was required to become or remain a county seat – a repository for the county's records plus a room where disputes could be heard and criminal trials conducted. Frontier towns in the plains had been known to steal the county seat by confiscating the county records, but that wasn't going to happen to Norton.

Lenora was unlike most small cities of western Kansas in that settlers arrived and formed a small town before the railroad arrived. By the time the railroad reached Lenora in 1882, the small community could boast about 230 residents. There the rails ended and a roundhouse turned westbound trains so they could return east. Local residents believed that construction of a rail link with the growing west was just around the corner although, in reality, the town's future had been stymied because no one ever would build a rail connection to the growing cities further west. Construction

22

started to extend a railroad west of Lenora but stopped before rails were laid. An engineer wrote W. W. Heatherington, president of the Central Trust Co., and proposed a 38-mile extension of the North Solomon line from Lenora to Hoxie so it would connect with the Union Pacific's Lincoln and Colorado Line. It would run from Lenora past New Almelo and Lucerne to Hoxie and cost about $10,000 per mile. The line was considered but never built. Several smaller communities such as New Almelo, Delvale and Oronoque clung to precarious existences.

~

The James McEnroe family lived south across the Solomon River between Lenora and New Almelo but less than a half mile from the Lunneys. James, the father, was born in New York state and had lived in Iowa before coming to Kansas in 1879. James' father, like Anna Lunney, was Irish-born. His wife Mary McEnroe had died several years earlier, leaving a young family of four sons and two daughters still at home with the father to raise them. Catherine, the eldest daughter, married Gabriel Dunlap, Anna Lunney's brother, which meant that the Lunneys and McEnroes were related as well as neighbors. Two older sons had left home earlier, and Eugene or Gene, the eldest on the farm, and his younger siblings remained with their father.

It seems apparent that the McEnroes felt the economic pain from the depressions of the early years more than the Lunneys and some of their neighbors. James had a mortgage on the McEnroe farm, and times had become so hard that he had difficulty making payments. James showed himself to be a good Catholic parishioner, passing the collection basket on Sundays at the St. Joseph Church. The McEnroe family, including Eugene, seemed to be well-liked. In his mid-twenties, Gene had reached an age where he should have left home, perhaps found a wife, made an effort to start his own farm and began raising a family. He hadn't. Maybe it was the Panic of '93, which had engulfed the nation and made it hard to start on one's own. And it was easier to stay at home under your father's roof when the nation's economy gave more pain than promise.

It wasn't because Gene was needed to work on the farm. Daniel, at age eighteen, and Patsey, younger at fifteen, were capable of doing most of the routine work. The family undoubtedly felt the loss of their mother Mary, who had died earlier, but daughter Ellen, at twenty-two, did most of the household work. Like Ellen Lunney, Ellen McEnroe had not found a husband. Sometimes it was wiser not to marry when times were so hard.

The McEnroe and Lunney families had sons nearly the same age, and the boys played together and frequently ate at each other's home, slept overnight and helped each other with the farm chores. Eugene tried, unsuccessfully, to court Ellen Lunney. Ellen had reached an age where she would be looking for a husband, but she firmly rejected the advances of young McEnroe. He tried to improve his looks by growing a mustache, perhaps for Ellen. Gene may have been popular with other young men his age, but he still did not appeal to Ellen.

While the children of the Lunney and McEnroe families had a lively social interchange, there is no evidence that the parents were close. The children might be able to skip across the small river separating the two farms. For the Lunneys parents to visit, they would have boarded a buggy and driven several miles to cross a small bridge before reaching the McEnroes. And it seemed apparent that the McEnroes, living in a house that was half sod and facing fiscal difficulties, would have been socially a notch or two below the wealthier Lunneys.

Yet the interwoven fabric of frontier life would tie the Lunneys, Dunlaps, Gilleeces and McEnroes during these early years on the prairie. In 1894, two of the families – the Lunneys and McEnroes – would become involved in an event that interrupted and changed lives of many in the small, isolated community in rural Norton County, Kansas.

The John Lunney family pictured not long before John Lunney's death in 1917. Seated from left: John Lunney Sr., Delena (Mrs. Robert McCrea), Anna and John (Jack) Jr.) Standing from left: Thomas, Mary (Mrs. J. C. Costello), Ellen (or Ella, Mrs. John Dwyer, as she later was known,) Rose (Mrs. T. A. Costello) and William.

Anna, who lived with several of her children after her husband's death, died in 1933. Note the similarity in the appearances of the three sons. (Photo courtesy of Caryl Finnerty.)

Three

The children shall inherit the earth.

By the summer of 1894, the children of the homesteaders were well on their way to reaping their heritage. John Lunney, in his late 50s, relied on his children to relieve the heavy burden of his farm work.

Ellen, in addition to her elementary school education, had the advantage of attending the county high school in Norton. At age nineteen, she had received a teaching certificate and already had taught in the neighborhood country schools. At that time these country schools, usually one or two rooms, had a two-month-long fall term and a three-month spring term. High school for the Lunney boys was almost out of the question because their father needed help at the farm. When she was at home, Ellen helped her mother Anna with the cooking and other household chores, including handling the milk produced by the farm's cows. While Ellen planned to teach school the following fall, finding a job was proving difficult because the depressed economy had left farmers with little money to hire school teachers.

Everything indicates that John Lunney was well-suited to farming and successful financially. One local history described Irish-born John Lunney in 1894: "One of the most prosperous farmers of the county, he owns 800 acres of land and is an extensive raiser of alfalfa. They have seven children, three boys and four girls."

John Lunney would have known the price of failure. He came to the United States from Ireland in 1862. He and his family survived the great Irish famine of 1846 and 1847 that was caused by the failure of the country's potato crop. Thousands of Irish fled the famine, many of them landing on America's shores. John would have been a nine-year-old boy when the ravishes of the terrible hunger began being felt, and he surely would have known the food shortages suffered by a starving nation. He must have been motivated strongly by a desire to never again experience what happened to the Irish in those years.

John joined his brother James, who had journeyed to America in 1847 and put down roots near Woodstock, Illinois. But younger brother John felt the lure of the frontier and continued on to Iowa. He later headed west again, this time finding a homestead southwest of Lenora in southwestern Norton County.

Anna Lunney gave birth to Ellen, their first-born, in a sod house, or dugout, along Marsh Creek. Western Kansas settlers without wood to build homes tunneled into

James Lunney, older brother of John, preceded John to America and put down his roots in Illinois, where he succeeded as a small–town businessman in Woodstock. Both James and John would have lived through the Irish potato famine. James came from County Fermanagh in 1847 and lived for a time with an uncle, Terrence McGee, one of Woodstock's pioneers. (Photo courtesy of Caryl Finnerty.)

the hillsides or built sod houses on the flat prairie, living like ground hogs with bugs, spiders and snakes. One early settler defined a sod house as dirt on all four walls, dirt on the floor and dirt on the ceiling with varmints choosing to share the roof space as they wished. Roofs customarily leaked when it rained. Pots and pans collected the drippings. When it rained, women sometimes cooked a meal under an umbrella held by someone else.

Dugouts in Kansas, probably not much different from the ones John and Anna Lunney lived in after their marriage. (Photo courtesy of Kansas State Historical Society, Topeka, Kansas.)

The writing of the song "Home on the Range" has been traced to 1910, but many early residents joked after hearing it of living in dugouts or "Holes in the Range."

Compared to those luckier pioneers in other states who could cut trees and build log cabins, the new occupants of the plains lived a rugged, difficult life that often depressed the entire family. Suicide was common. Shootings were frequent. Husbands or wives sometimes ended the pain by killing their entire families. The discontented often loaded the prairie schooner again and headed back east. The plains were not for everyone.

By 1874 Norton County, Kansas, and much of that great span of plains that stretched from Canada to Mexico, stood on the cusp of America's western frontier. It was here that the United States Army and the march of pioneers were finishing clearing the land of Indians and buffalo, bringing a new type of culture and a civilization of farms and small towns to a barren land. The western Kansas frontier was far from unique since other pioneers had been marching westward and opening land to agriculture for more than a hundred years. Yet this frontier nevertheless was different.

Nobody described the land as an eden, like far-off Oregon or California. The region lacked water. Plants, animals and the humans occupying the dry prairie had to adapt to this condition. In some years the amount of rainfall would prove sufficient to grow crops. Some years it was not. About the time the farmers felt prosperous and enjoyed the fruits of their labors, a year or more of parching drought seemed to follow. Settlers in Illinois, Iowa and Indiana had come west with boats, canoes and axes. None of these proved necessary in western Kansas. John Lunney had no ax and few tools but what he borrowed from George Miller, a friendly neighbor who helped him clear the land.

Tornadoes, or cyclones, often unfurled their wrath on the Kansas plains. Winters had their winds, too, and if accompanied by moisture, the result could be a volley of cold, blinding, blowing snow that paralyzed the countryside for days.

Such weather on the prairie kept trees from growing, resulting in a shortage of wood for settlers who wanted to build homes, barns and towns. Some trees lined the area's rivers and streams, but their branches usually had been picked clean by buffalo. Sometimes grasshoppers arrived and ate what the buffalo missed.

~

The household of John and Anna Lunney frequently included John McKeniff, a twenty-five-year-old nephew of John Lunney. John McKeniff and his older brother Hugh were sons of John Lunney's sister, Catherine McKeniff, who lived in County Cavan, Ireland. The sons immigrated to the United States under the sponsorship of John Lunney. Hugh had homesteaded in a soddie across the Solomon River. John McKeniff worked as a hired hand but frequently stayed with the Lunneys. The neighbors believed John McKeniff had a romantic crush on Ellen Lunney, but they did not seem to have any evidence that Ellen reciprocated in the relationship. Yet, there was plenty of neighborhood gossip speculating what the relationship was.

Tom and fifteen-year-old Will had finished their schooling, which meant a maximum of eight years in a rural schoolhouse. Tom, at seventeen, had reached the age where he could do most of the routine farm work. Willie assisted in the daily chores of milking the cows, herding them to pasture in the morning and back to the barn in the evening, and feeding the hogs that nearly every farm raised for its own consumption. With the railroads providing a national market, Kansas was becoming the nation's wheat field, but for local consumption corn still reigned as king. It was fed to animals, particularly swine, and many a rural family survived by growing corn and raising hogs. Farm families frequently depended on pork as their main meat in their early days on the prairie.

Every year farmers produced more winter wheat, and they would continue to do so throughout the last years of the nineteenth century. The state Board of Agriculture reported that Kansans grew twice or three times as much corn as wheat. But this was misleading because wheat-growing was becoming concentrated in the arid western part of the state. Wheat became the main cash crop in western Kansas about 1880, and a few wet years encouraged growing even more of the grain. Farmers believed that soon the new railroads would connect these rural fields of grain to a national or regional market that demanded larger quantities of wheat and flour. At times the railroads, encouraging farmers to grow more for a national market, loaned seed wheat to farmers along their lines. But wheat yields depended on weather and rain. Precipitation in Kansas tends to fall mainly in the winter and spring, and those are the months when winter wheat requires moisture to produce the summer's golden fields of grain. Some years rain fell and the farmers prospered. In other years the rain clouds never appeared and the farm families would have starved if not for credit from local merchants in the small market towns that served them.

~

Farm life had grown easier since John and Anna Lunney homesteaded in the 1870s. Historian Homer E. Socolofsky gave this description of farm life in 1876:

> Most farm homes, too small for the family, were lacking in elementary sanitary conditions, and were infested with insect pests of various kinds. Fresh, clean water was nowhere to be found in many farm homes – the inevitable rain barrel invariably contained polluted water. Homes were isolated from most neighbors, adding to the loneliness of farm women. Faced with never ending household and farm drudgery, the demands of laundry, kitchen, stove, a vegetable garden and a growing family, many a young country wife quickly lost the bloom of good health and physical attractiveness.

The Lunneys suffered but held on during their early years on the east bank of Marsh Creek, west of the twin mounds, two tall cones that rose above the countryside and served as landmarks. They endured the hot summer of 1874 but in August, when the corn was tasseling, a horde of grasshoppers descended. They darkened the afternoon like a storm cloud. The shirr of wings sounded like wind. They devoured every growing thing. Corn, grass, gardens and even the bark on the trees. They ate holes in ladies' dresses. They cut a swath 250 miles wide and ate their way through several states, consuming all things edible on 5,000 square miles of farmland at a sitting. The third day they flew away in a northeasterly direction. The people saved their potatoes and carrots, but that was about all.

The grasshoppers attack of 1874 was not the only havoc that beset the early settlers.

John Hickert told the story of what happened to the John Lunney family during the last buffalo run in the fall of 1876. "The year had been good to John and his young family. He hand-cut and shocked the corn, filled a grass-lined pit with vegetables for the winter, and he was happy to have all these good crops. His happiness was of a short duration," Hickert, an early resident, related.

> One moonlit evening in October they heard a very unusual rumbling sound. Looking out they saw an immense herd of buffalo on its annual trek south for the winter. Luckily their dugout was in a heavily wooded area, and this was a protection. The run lasted for thirty-six hours. Mr. Lunney's corn shocks had been pulverized and mashed potatoes, turnips, carrots and cabbage oozed up through the hay covering the vegetable pit. In these migrations the younger buffalo calves were unable to keep up with the herds. The Lunneys and their neighbors gathered up twenty-four of these calves and wintered them. The following spring a railroad man from WaKeeney purchased them for twenty dollars each. This was their first cash income.

Like the constancy of the winds on the prairie, change came with the turn of the calendar. By 1894 the region had been populated by a fast-growing civilization of farms and small towns that sprouted dramatically on the plains. Life changed from a subsistence, hand-to-mouth existence to a more complex market economy. The Lunneys sold meat, milk, vegetables and eggs in Lenora. Grocers often tried to pay the farmers in goods but allowed their customers to charge what they needed.

There is no indication that the Lunneys or other Catholic families played much of a role in what happened in nearby Lenora, a Protestant town. The Catholics decided it was better to keep to themselves unless they needed to venture to town for business purposes such as taking out a loan, selling produce or buying food or clothing. Lenora had a newspaper during many of its early years that sought out personal items about families in town or the close-in countryside, but the Lunney name seldom appears. Nor do most of the other Irish families (Gabe Dunlap's name was noted at least once) who seemed content to huddle in a communal-type existence and let the outside world solve its own problems. It would be left for the children of the homesteaders and early settlers to enter the public life of their communities.

The urbanization of the American plains saw the growth of thousands of small towns across the prairie. The free range ended, fenced with barbed wire into plots of farm or pasture land. Anna Lunney could buy a variety of new foods such as bananas and oysters from the town grocers. She could buy ready-to-wear clothing from stores advertising clothing for men, women and children. Roads had been improved. Telephones and electricity would come soon to the area, which would change it even more.

⁓

The Lunney's closest neighbors, the McEnroes, lived across the Solomon River. Never a fast-flowing river, the North Branch of the Solomon customarily produced a flow of water even in summer. During dry summers the streamflow often was not more than a trickle. But even high water didn't slow the lively social interchange between the Lunneys and McEnroes. The Lunney and McEnroe boys scampered easily across the river, climbed through the barb wire fences and soon stood at the other family's doorstep. Eugene McEnroe, the eldest child at home, was twenty-six. He was at an age that he would have thought of marrying and starting a family. His older brothers James, Jr., and William, had departed the crowded McEnroe home, married and started families.

⁓

Tuesday, July 24, 1894

The morning began as a typically sunny day on the Lunney farm. The searing sun already had burned most of the area's corn crop. No ears or tassels of corn would appear this year on much of the burned stalks. Instead, the stalks were being cut early and fed to the pigs. Any wheat produced had been harvested earlier in the month.

Sometime during Tuesday morning, John and Anna Lunney decided to visit Anna's sister and her family, the McKennas, who lived ten miles to the west on a farm a mile from the small town of Allison, located in Decatur County, which bordered Norton County on the west. Anna's sister Sarah had married Edward McKenna, and they and their family lived in a house along the Solomon River. Because of the distance, John and Anna decided to take all the young Lunney children – John (Jack) Jr., Mary, Rose and Delena. Ellen, Tom and Will needed to stay and do routine farm chores.

The parents told Ellen, Tom and Will that the length of the trip might require them to stay overnight. If the travelers did not return by nightfall, assume they were spending the night with the McKennas, John and Anna told the older children. Ellen asked Mary to stay home with her, but Mary wanted to go with the rest of the family to visit the McKennas, who had several children of their own. The Lunneys boarded their wagon and headed west down the river road about fourteen miles to visit the McKennas.

Later in the afternoon two McEnroe brothers, Eugene and Patsey, appeared at the Lunneys, and they and Tom went to cut corn at a field farmed by the McEnroes. Nothing unusual. Later Dan came and ate supper with the three Lunneys, which everyone later said was not unusual either, and after the meal Patsey came over. Dan and Patsey helped the Lunneys with the milking and chores.

Anyone observing the scene would see the five young men of two families closely interlocked in their activities. Tom Lunney joined Gene and Patsey McEnroe in cutting their dead corn. Then Dan McEnroe, after appearing for dinner at the Lunneys, helped Tom and Willie with the Lunney's chores.

By ten o'clock, it had become apparent that the traveling Lunneys would not return that evening. Ellen said as much when she went to the pump for water before going to bed. She told her brothers, as well as Dan and Patsy McEnroe, who were at the Lunneys. Then Ellen went to bed.

And to sleep.

Four

Wednesday, July 25, 1894.

The morning sun bore into the parched plain, darkening its brown vegetation another shade. A spring wagon, pulled by two strong black horses, rolled slowly eastward down the river road. The horses made good time along the flat route and carried the wagon's cargo of two adults and four children to their homecoming. The wagon pulled into the farmyard but met an unexpected silence. The Lunneys anticipated a greeting welcoming the family back to the farm, but the grounds were quiet. Not even a dog barked.

Lanky Tom Lunney was the first to emerge from the house. His father asked if everything was all right. Then John Lunney saw his fifteen-year-old son Will walking slowly toward him. Will was sobbing. Then he noticed Tom had been crying.

What was wrong? John Lunney asked a second time.

You soon will know, Tom answered. What happened was not appropriate to discuss in front of the young children.

Then John McKeniff, almost a member of the family, appeared. He too seemed to have been crying.

The Lunneys, returning from an overnight visit to Anna's Lunney's sister and her family, soon learned what occurred in the nighttime of their absence. Ellen, tearful and shaken, told her mother the story: About midnight or shortly thereafter she awakened from a sound sleep to find a man with his hand over her mouth. He probed, he pushed beneath her nightgown. She cried and tried to scream. His hand tightened on her mouth. She couldn't scream. She could hardly move.

The intruder finished his business. Ellen could not rise for several moments. When she did she looked outside and saw the man walking quickly along the corn cribs, staying away from the granary where her two brothers Tom and Will slept in the summer's night heat.

Her father asked, could she see who it was?

Ellen had no difficulty seeing her assailant in the bright moonlight. She had known who it was even before the moonbeams gave him away. It was Eugene. Gene McEnroe. Their neighbor. A relative since Catherine McEnroe, Gene's sister, had married one of Anna Dunlap Lunney's brothers. A shitpot Gene McEnroe was. A bastard, too lazy to go out and start his own farm, his own family. He may have been well-liked, but it was because he spent so much time in the pool hall with the other loafers. The family cursed Gene McEnroe. For Ellen's skinned knees. For her bloody drawers. For the broken latch on the screen door. Mostly for the rape, the loss of her chastity.

Last night, after Ellen had roused the two boys, Tom had got out the shotgun and took the dogs down to the river. He fired off the gun. Three times. A warning for the McEnroes not to come back across the river. Not to molest Ellen any more. The gunshots signaled the end of the close relationship between the two families. Gene McEnroe had ripped it asunder. Never again would the shiftless McEnroe boys, adrift with nothing to do, be welcome at the Lunney home.

John Lunney needed time to think. To do the morning chores that the boys had neglected. To quiet his daughter Ellen who couldn't stop crying. The Irish liked to keep disputes in the family, or at least in the neighborhood, but this was a rape, a crime. Twenty years ago he would have taken a shotgun, walked across the river and dealt with Gene and his family. But the law had come to western Kansas. He could have gotten away with shooting a man for raping his daughter twenty years ago, but not now, in 1894. Too much had happened, too much had changed since Ellen was born.

Such was the decision, the most important to face John Lunney in years. If the Lunneys filed a complaint against Gene McEnroe, it would amount to a declaration to all that his daughter had been raped, despoiled, damaged. Would other men still consider her as a bride? Probably not. Men wanted to think that their wives were virgins, and a rape would raise a terrible cloud over Ellen. She may have to leave the community, to find a new home where her history wasn't known.

But the aging, white-haired farmer could think later about those choices. John Lunney needed to make a decision, and he soon realized the course of action he must take. He must have Gene McEnroe arrested for the rape of his oldest child.

But before long another McEnroe boy, eighteen-year-old Dan McEnroe appeared, coming up from the riverbank from the direction of his home. Normally talkative, Dan McEnroe said little. He hung around, sniffing the air like a bird dog trying to determine if life on the north side of the Solomon River still existed the same as it was the last time he was there. The last time, of course, had been the previous night before the rape. Was his morning visit to judge the reaction of the Lunneys? Soon, avoided by the young Lunney boys as well as the elders, he left, moving quietly back across the river toward his own home.

Dan had no difficulty understanding the silent message. He no longer was welcome at the Lunneys. Emotions ran raw in the Lunney farmyard. Even the Lunney dogs seem to growl at the young Dan, a familiar face. But Gene was Dan's older brother, and Dan and Patsy loved him and sometimes stood in awe at his wisdom and his knowledge of the outside world. The Lunneys saw Dan as a scout surveying the farm to see what had changed since last night.

John Lunney again harnessed and hitched the horses and prepared for another trip, this one not as pleasant as the visit to relatives upriver. John and his daughter Ellen soon moved down the road to the home of Squire D. H. Thuma, who lived a few miles northeast.

But Thuma, the justice of the peace, was not at home. John and Ellen again boarded the wagon and headed to the home of Squire

W. H. Hendricks, another justice of the peace, who lived in Lenora. The charge should be listed as rape, said John Lunney, and he wanted Gene McEnroe arrested.

On Thursday, July twenty-six, Squire Hendricks did his sworn duty. He sent E. J. Muzzy, Lenora's constable, to the McEnroe home to arrest Eugene. His bail was set at $1,000, but no one had that kind of money, least of all the McEnroes, who were in danger of losing their farm over a debt of a few hundred dollars. Then it was decided that young Gabe Dunlap, Anna Lunney's brother but recently married into the McEnroe family, would guarantee the bond with his signature. Ellen's own uncle! Gene McEnroe went free. A hearing was set on the Lunney complaint for July thirty-one, a week after the nighttime of Ellen Lunney's horror.

$\sim$

Ellen spent much of the next week crying. Guests shuffled through the Lunney's front door to pay their respects or because they heard the story and curiosity had got the better of them. They wanted to know what had happened. Almost all the guests became worried about Ellen after seeing her. They saw her frequently break down, sobbing and unable to stop. She was in bad shape.

A day later – or was it two days – Ellen, crying and afraid, called to her mother. She had been certain she saw Gene McEnroe hacking away at dead corn in a field near their house. Wasn't McEnroe supposed to be in jail? How could they let Gene go free after he committed his terrible crime upon her body? Didn't they consider the rape a serious crime against her? She didn't know what to do.

Anna looked to see if Eugene was cutting corn. She saw someone but could not tell which McEnroe boy it was. Everyone said the Lunney sons all looked alike. The McEnroe boys looked a lot alike, too. Maybe Eugene was cutting fodder in Ellen's view. Maybe it wasn't Eugene. Anna's eyes weren't as good as they once had been. Maybe Ellen had been crying so much she was seeing things. Ellen had been telling visitors, those she knew well enough to speak to, that she wished she were dead. She wished Gene had killed her, not just wounded her for eternity.

~

For Gene McEnroe, the week before the hearing was much like any other week. He helped around the house, but he had little to do. As the oldest son at home, he passed off some of the routine chores to his brothers, Dan and Patsey. They had become old enough to do most anything that needed to be done. Got to keep them busy. Work was good for them.

It was difficult for Gene McEnroe to keep busy. He could not find a job. He could climb on his horse and go to Lenora and loiter on the streets or visit the pool hall and, if he had any money, find a card game or drink beer. Below a Lenora grocery and dry goods store lay a cool basement card parlor. One had to be careful. Some of the young men still carried revolvers. Not that they needed a pistol in a holster on their hip. A pistol showed they were not to be trifled with. Gene should not have had much trouble. He was popular with folks in town. Besides, although he had not grown tall, he had proven himself strong for his size. He would have done well for himself in Lenora's pool hall and card room.

Gene McEnroe's main problem was a lack of money in his own pocket. The same was true for the community, state and nation generally. Nobody had much money. The nation had become snarled in a severe depression, which started as the Panic of 1893 when the stock market collapsed and banks began closing their doors.

By the early 1890s many of the settlers were moving out of western Kansas to any place that sounded better. The regional economy began its collapse as far back as 1888. "All that had gone up, it seemed, as dramatically went down," said historian Craig Miner. "The rain stopped, the wind and snow started, population dropped, crops failed, credit tightened, railroad companies withdrew, the land-office business shriveled, cattlemen gave up, irrigation ditches dried up, sugar mills burned up, towns had safes full of worthless bonds to give away, and farm families found that suddenly it was 1880 again." News reporters from the East came to western Kansas to tell about the evacuation of settlers and the return of the "Great American Desert." Maybe the desert hadn't been conquered by civilization after all.

Wagons daily left the frontier and headed elsewhere bearing signs such as "In God we trusted, in Kansas we busted." The whole nation seemed to have busted. President Grover Cleveland had been warned by friendly financiers of a pending economic panic so serious that it could force the nation off the gold standard. The Panic of 1893 saw many railroads fall into bankruptcy, financial houses and trusts collapse, and a run began on the banks, many which closed their doors. Crop prices fell. Stock prices declined. The nation's gold reserves shrunk. By 1894 the nation had plunged into a full-fledged depression.

President Grover Cleveland did not know what to do, so he went fishing. Cleveland had become a serious angler and fished whenever he could. Frequently he was absent from the White House or wherever else he was living as he scurried off to fishing holes on the Potomac, boating and fishing excursions on Chesapeake Bay and to his vacation home on Massachusetts' Buzzards Bay. While Americans feared the vultures of death, Cleveland found solace with friends practicing his angling technique on the waters of Buzzards Bay.

Cleveland, known for his honesty, had risen in politics as a reform mayor of Buffalo, New York, and then became the governor of New York before he reached the presidency. He was a gruff, recently married bachelor who delighted in telling long, humorous stories and frolicking with his nieces and nephews, who called the heavy man "Jumbo." He had so little privacy in the White House, and had been hounded so badly by the sensational press of the day, that he essentially moved out of the executive's quarters after he married. He and his wife lived on a twenty-three-acre farm several miles north of the White House near where the National Cathedral later would stand. Overwhelmed by the enormity of the nation's problems, the celebrated reformer from Buffalo surrendered. Cleveland barely presided over the office during the last two years of his presidency. But maybe fishing wasn't a bad way to spend one's time in the heat of a hot, humid Washington, D. C., summer.

∾

One of the more remarkable reactions to the Panic of '93 was the birth of so-called industrial armies, such as Coxey's Army, that began a march on Washington, D.C., in hopes of gaining the attention of the nation. Thanks to the growth of a national journalism that quickly transmitted news from coast to coast via the telegraph and the mail, the country learned about a group of roving armies from the western and midwestern states marching, or riding, to Washington to lay their protest at the foot of those who, if not responsible, were capable of doing something about it! "To call them an army of 'bums, tramps and vagabonds,' as some commentators were doing, was a complete misrepresentation," said Ray Stannard Baker, a journalist traveling with the army. "A considerable proportion were genuine farmers and workingmen whose only offense was the fact that they could not buy or rent land – having no money – or find a job at which they could earn a living." Sympathetic senators and congressmen talked about public works projects, mainly road building or digging irrigation ditches. Frederick Jackson Turner spoke about the problem being the end of the frontier, where no longer could the west "furnish a new field of opportunity, a gate of escape from the bondage of the past."

Jacob Coxey's Army started in Ohio in the spring of 1894, but long before Coxey and his rag-tag unemployed workers reached the District of Columbia, the nation knew what was happening by simply reading the newspaper stories of reporters like Jack London accompanying the armies. In fact, a bunch of armies, not just one, headed to Washington, and most did not plan on walking all the way. They began stealing railroad trains. Unemployed men, and a few women, hijacked more than fifty trains, many from as far west as California, Oregon, Washington state and Montana. Friendly populist governors such as those in Oregon, Kansas and Colorado did little to prevent the thievery of trains even if they did not encourage it openly.

John Sherman Sanders led a group of miners who commandeered a Missouri Pacific train at Pueblo, Colorado, in May 1894 and ran it east to Scott City, Kansas, ninety miles south of Lenora. Both Colorado and Kansas governors supported agrarian protest, and neither gave the railroad much help. Railroad attorneys finally decided that anyone fooling with a train in interstate commerce was interfering with the U. S. mail, and that got the attention of a federal judge in Kansas. The judge told the railroad to do what it needed to do, and the railroad tore up its own track to stop the train. Sanders and his men surrendered peaceably. Populist Governor Lorenzo Lewelling of Kansas transported the hijackers to Fort Leavenworth where they were fed military rations and housed in tents, the best treatment they had received in weeks. Officials at the fort allowed the men to box and to fish for recreation and to lie in the warm sun. Sanders became a lecturer for the populists and later courted and married the daughter of an official of the Kansas state prison in nearby Lansing. Some industrial army protesters who reached Washington were arrested for trespassing on federal property, which pretty much ended the first nationally organized protest march on the nation's capital.

It did not end the economic plight of a nation of hungry, homeless and out-of-work people. Eugene McEnroe had his father's roof over his head, but many had lost their homes and had no where to go. The terrible times spawned a political protest, populism, that had many of its roots in the Kansas sod.

∽

In the days after Ellen Lunney's rape, it seems probable that the adults – at least Ellen and her parents and possibly Tom, the eldest son – would have discussed what to do. Ellen told everyone she thought her life was ruined, that everyone would consider her an unchaste, fallen woman. Ellen believed that carrying the burden of her lost womanhood would detract from her ability to attract a husband and live a normal life. A popular marital guide in the 1890s advised young women that true love lasted a lifetime, and chastity should be used as the only foolproof method to avoid inconvenient pregnancies. Sex between married persons was normal but for pro-creation. "In every civilized community, thousands live in celibacy, many from from necessity, many from choice," said the marital guide.

The question, never fully resolved, was whether the Lunneys collectively planned the next step that occurred, whether they conspired and decided to retaliate against their neighbors, the McEnroes, and the thief of Ellen's virtue, Eugene McEnroe.

This much is known: at some point in the week between the rape and the hearing on July 31, Ellen asked her brother Tom to buy her a pistol. Tom and John McKeniff went to Lenora to purchase a revolver. Somehow Tom had sufficient money to buy a six-shooter for his sister. Did the parents provide those funds, about five dollars? Tom later would say he had his father's permission to take money from the old man's pants pockets when he needed it. But these were hard times. Could Tom have possibly taken five dollars from his father's pocket without John Lunney knowing it?

It stretches the imagination to think John Lunney did not know that a revolver had been bought. What did old man Lunney think the pistol for, scaring away crows? Or the McEnroe boys?

The Lunneys house was crowded with the large family. Ellen would say later that she placed the pistol in a family bureau drawer for safe-keeping. No one supposedly noticed the revolver's presence. Brother Tom later admitted he gave her basic instruction in how to fire the weapon although she could not hit a tree directly in front of her. But no one in the family seemed to notice the sound of nearby gunfire, or so they would say later.

Suspicious, everyone would say. More than a little suspicious.

Five

A terrible tragedy took place on Tuesday, in a school house near Lenora, where an examination was about to take place wherein Ellen Lunney was plaintiff, charging Eugene McEnroe with an assault upon her person one night a short time ago while she was at home alone. Between forty and fifty people had gathered to listen to the examination and were waiting for the arrival of the attorneys from Norton. Just before their arrival, Miss Lunney stepped into the school room and locating young McEnroe, approached him to the left and rear and fired four shots into his body, killing him almost instantly. Miss Lunney was placed under arrest as was also her cousin John McKeniff, as accessory. We do not believe it would be proper for us to comment upon this case. It will come before the court for investigation when the truth will probably be brought out and given to the public. It is a sad affair to say the least, where two or more young lives are blasted. Miss Lunney was a county graduate about two weeks ago.

Norton Courier, *August 2, 1894.*

Norton, the county seat of Norton County, lies in the Prairie Dog Valley halfway between Kansas City and Denver. Once past Norton, travelers headed west for Colorado's capital would not see a town Norton's size until reaching Denver and its surrounding communities. Towns got farther apart and smaller as one moved west of the 100th meridian, the imaginary but important demarcation which lay a few miles west of Norton.

Norton County appeared at least twice in writing about the early plains. Explorer John C. Fremont passed by during his 1843 trip through the region and called the creek that ran through the middle of the county the Prairie Dog, the name it still bears, because of the large number of the bothersome rodents inhabiting the neighborhood. Then, in 1859, Horace Greeley, the famous *New York Tribune* editor, passed through Norton County on a stagecoach trip west enroute to California. Historians believe Greeley camped on the west edge of what now is the city of Norton. Greeley commented in his letters on the thousands of buffalo and the hunters pursuing them, but he said settlement in 1859 had not progressed west much beyond Junction City, 200 miles to the east. Greeley said he was "near the heart of the buffalo region" when he was along the Solomon and Prairie Dog rivers.

"The herbage hereabout is nearly all the short, strong grass known as the buffalo-grass, and is closely fed down; we are far beyond the stakes of the land surveyor – beyond the usual haunts of white men," Greeley wrote. "The country for miles on either hand seemed quite black" with buffalo. He estimated his stage must have passed a million or more of the placid animals. Greeley and his party camped along the Prairie Dog Creek on May 31, 1859, and by that time his concern was warring Indians rather than roaming buffalo. He wrote of sheets of falling rain and soil washing away. "It needs to be timbered before it can be fit for the habitation of civilized man," Greeley said of the countryside, a dozen years before John Lunney and the Dunlaps would homestead the same, sparse, nearly timber-less land in the southwestern party of the new county.

Norton County is located in what was known before the U. S. Civil War as the "Great American Desert." Settlers were advised to bypass the land lying west of what had been cultivated along the Missouri River Valley, eastern Kansas or certainly the 100th Meridian. Even the early maps listed this largely unexplored low-rainfall area that would be difficult to farm as a desert. Major Stephen H. Long, after his expedition of 1819-1820, described the American heartland's desert as "almost wholly unfit for cultivation, and of course uninhabitable by a people depending upon agriculture for their subsistence."

Most of the early pathfinders, trappers, explorers, missionaries and land settlers found their way past Norton County without much difficulty. The two primary routes from Kansas City, Independence or Westport, Missouri, lay to the north and south. By the 1840s when the early wagons loaded with pioneers headed west, usually for California or the Oregon territory, they most often departed from the main outfitting settlements of Independence or Westport or later from Leavenworth and Atchison, Kansas. The main travel route took them west across the Kansas border for about forty miles. Here the road split, the Santa Fe Trail winding southwesterly to what would become the Oklahoma panhandle and eventually New Mexico or beyond to California.

If the prairie schooners traveled the northern overland trail, they continued their route on the south side of the Kansas River until they came to where they could ford. Then the wagons followed the north bank of the river for a time before proceeding northwest along the Big Blue River near where the town of Marysville now is located and headed toward Nebraska's Platte River. Within a few years several other trails intersected this nineteenth century highway, coming from the new Missouri River communities of Leavenworth, Atchison and St. Joseph. The route along the south side of the Platte – another trail, the Mormon Trail, ran to the north of the Platte – bore many names, the Platte Trail, the Emigrant Trail, Oregon Trail, Overland Trail. James Clyman, a trapper and trail traveler, wrote in his diary that it was the Oregon Trace. Blazers of the route described the unnavigable Platte River as being "a mile wide and an inch deep" and filled with dangerous sand that sometimes in wet weather would suck down horses or a wagon that ventured too close to its oozing, meandering channels, which looked easy to cross but could prove treacherous to the unwary. The road to Oregon came within fifty miles of Norton County, which began filling with settlers in the 1870s, thirty years after the wagon trains started moving along the Platte River.

By 1894 almost all the land in the area had been homesteaded. Just a year before a young Frederick Jackson Turner had stood before the American Historical Association in Chicago and said that the free land in the West could explain the young nation's development, and that the days of western expansion had ended because the frontier had closed with uncertain consequences for America's future.

Frederick Jackson Turner's end-of-the-frontier thesis did not go over well when he presented it at the World's Columbian Exposition in Chicago, which was celebrating the 400th anniversary of the discovery of America. This did not seem to bother Turner, a self-promoter unbound by the cloisters of academic life. He purchased reprints of his speech and distributed them to his academic colleagues and other opinion makers in America. In short, his thesis was not self-evident to anyone at the time, and it passed almost unnoticed until Turner himself publicized what he had said and described the importance of his words.

One reason Turner's ideas missed connecting immediately was because much of the American West still remained unsettled, or sparsely settled. In the previous five years Idaho, Wyoming, Washington, Montana and North and South Dakota had become states, and Oklahoma had been opened to non-Indian settlement. Hawaii did not become a republic until 1893, Alaska remained unsettled and Utah, Oklahoma, Arizona, New Mexico and Nevada remained years away from statehood.

Turner may have been right in 1893 that the western expansion explained America's development, but he wasn't quite correct that the frontier had closed. At least many of the dislocated folk of the western plain still believed that the sparsely settled west still offered, if not free land, plenty of opportunity when things got bad enough to pull up stakes and find another home on the range.

And in 1894, plenty of Kansans felt it was time to pack up and move along because hard times had severely depressed Norton County and the rest of the country. Three counties stood between Norton and Colorado, and many headed in that direction, or back east where they came from a few years earlier. Plenty of empty land seemed to beckon.

$\sim$

The Norton County Courthouse with wagons lining the street. The courthouse became the scene of the Lunney trial in 1894. In 1893 and 1894 the sheriff sold many foreclosed farm properties from the building's steps. The Panic of 1893 forced many of the farms into foreclosure and scattered their occupants. (Photo courtesy of Kansas State Historical Society, Topeka.)

Everyone said the finest building in growing Norton had to be the county courthouse, which stood on the square in the center of the business district. The size of the courthouse was meant to show authority. Its three stories and cupola housed the three county commissioners, other county officials and the district attorney, C. D. Jones. Small businesses in wooden one- and two-story buildings lined the blocks facing the courthouse although imported brick had started appearing in the new storefronts. Citizens with county business tied their horses and left their carriages in the street facing the courthouse.

C. D. Jones, "The Colonel," who as county attorney was the lead prosecutor in the Ellen Lunney murder trial. (Photo from F. M. Lockard, *The History of the Early Settlement of Norton County, Kansas.*)

Charles Douglas Jones was serving his first term as prosecutor. Thin, he parted his straight brown hair on the left; a full mustache below made his face seem fuller. The wiry, short lawyer had celebrated his forty-sixth birthday in July. Born in Covington, Indiana, Charles was the son of a physician who had been one of Indiana's pioneers, C. V. Jones. At age seventeen young Jones entered Asbury University, later known as DePauw University, at Green Castle, Indiana, intending to become a school teacher. He graduated in 1871 and soon after was elected superintendent of the public schools of Williamsport, Indiana, a position he held for two years. But another profession beckoned and he made a rapid career change. He studied law, and in 1874 he was elected prosecuting attorney of White and Tippecanoe counties in Indiana. Jones decided to participate in Republican Party politics because he saw serving in public office as a possibility in his future, and he remained active in the party for the rest of his life. In 1885, when times were prosperous in the new towns of the plains, he and his wife moved to Norton County. A staunch Methodist, he stayed active in his church, the Republican Party and the Sons of Veterans, which gave him the honorary title of lieutenant colonel, and a year later in 1890 as colonel. He married Lucy Reed and the couple had five living children. Three more did not survive childhood.

They called Jones "the Colonel," an honorary title given because of his activity in the Sons of Veterans, which wanted the new generation to remember the Civil War of thirty years past.

In his job as Norton County attorney, the Colonel was deluged by land foreclosures. Because of the depressed economy, many owners of farms and homes could not meet their financial obligations, which left Jones and Sheriff George R. Betterton to foreclose on them and pass the property on to creditors. The law left them no choice: they sold several properties every week on the courthouse steps. In addition, Jones was constantly called into court to deal with a large number of criminal cases.

Now he had a new case on his hands. The State vs. Ellen Lunney, her brother Tom and a cousin named John McKeniff. To him it seemed like an open and shut case. He would dispose of it as soon as possible and bring the full authority of the state down on this young killer, a farm girl. Even if she had been raped, she had no right to shoot the young man, this McEnroe boy, in cold blood. The Colonel would remove her excuse of rape as the basis for a revenge killing. The law could make exceptions for self-defense, common in western courtrooms, but how could she claim she was defending herself a week after her rape?

And, since he was seeking reelection, Jones probably viewed the sensational Lunney trial as an opportunity to keep his name in the news in the weeks before voting in November. The Lunney case was attracting a lot of attention in Norton and Lenora, the county's third largest town. By the trial's end, everyone would know the name of the county's district attorney. Prosecuting a murder trial was far better than foreclosing on poor farmers for a district attorney seeking approval of the voters.

At first Jones also had charged the mother, Anna Lunney, but he soon dropped that idea because evidence of her involvement was slim. Ellen and Tom Lunney and the McKeniff lad seemed sufficient. The two boys apparently had purchased the murder weapon and, the way Jones saw it, tried to flee with Ellen after the shooting at the school. Local constables had stopped them. Jones had Ellen taken to jail, but that seemed awkward for everyone so he had

The warrant for the arrest of Ellen Lunney, John McKeniffe (name misspelled) and Thomas Lunney issued August 4, 1894, by Justice of the Peace D. H. Thuma and Constable E. H. Darnell and signed by Sheriff George R. Betterton. Note that the warrant originally bore Anne Lunney's name, but it was stricken. Darnell's fees for the service amounted to $1.55 and Thuma's to $1.30. (Warrant from Norton County Clerk's files.)

In the Court of D. H. Thuma a Justice
of the Peace in and for Lenora Township
Norton County. State of Kansas.

The State of Kansas }
vs } Complaint
Ellen Lunny. John McKuiffe
Thomas Lunny. and Ann Lunny }

Norton County. }
State of Kansas } ss

Charles D Jones
James McEnroe being first duly sworn
upon his oath says that on the 21st day
of July 1894. at the County of Norton and
State of Kansas. Ellen Lunny. John Mc
Kuiffe. Thomas Lunny and Ann Lunny
then and there being, with the wrongful, unlawful, malicious, felonious, deliberate
and premeditated intent to kill and
murder one Eugene McEnroe then and
there being. did then and there intentionally, feloniously. deliberately. willfully,
premeditatedly. and with malice aforethought
kill and murder the said Eugene McEnroe
by shooting him the said Eugene McEnroe

The first page of the complaint filed by D. H. Thuma, the local justice of the
peace, that charged four persons in the murder of Eugene McEnroe.
(Complaint from Norton County Clerk's files.)

lodged her at Sheriff Betterton's home. Now she seemed unlikely to flee since her brother and the McKeniff kid had been locked up.

Ellen must have been driven to distress when she saw how the county attorney handled her case. She, and her family, would have been outraged by Jones telling people that her rape never caused the crime. How could they treat the rape so lightly, letting Gene McEnroe out to cut corn in her own view as though nothing had happened? Nothing? The rape had changed her life and placed a mortgage on her future.

The Lunneys prepared to contest the case vigorously and hired Lafayette H. Thompson as their defense attorney. Lafe Thompson was the best-known lawyer in Norton County. He had served three, two-year terms as county attorney, the first in 1880. Not only had Thompson gained wide recognition in the county but he had managed to hang on to a private office in the county courthouse, and he bought newspaper advertising trumpeting the location as a convenience to anyone needing legal services. Norton's small legal community constantly saw its members on both sides of criminal and civil cases. All the lawyers knew each other well, socialized with their colleagues' families and often could predict what another lawyer would do. Norton wasn't a large town.

When Jones became county attorney in 1892, he defeated Ledru H. Wilder by four votes. Wilder had defeated Lafayette Thompson two years earlier by 330 votes. Because of his heavy workload, Jones hired Ledru Wilder as a second attorney to help the state in its prosecution in the Lunney case. To tighten the knot of how well these small-town attorneys knew each other, Jones and Thompson formerly worked as partners in a law firm. Both had become active in Republican politics. In fact, the two were seeking office in the summer of 1894, Thompson for state representative and Jones for reelection as county attorney. They frequently appeared together on the same political stage. They knew each other so well that perhaps it was their close friendship that persuaded both men to bring in an additional lawyer on each side.

Lafayette Thompson was not a bad country lawyer. The tall,

lanky man had been a journalist, teacher, miller and merchant before deciding on practicing law. He spoke in short phrases as if his thoughts were being formulated in his head and he wanted to place them before his audience before they disappeared.

Thompson's personal history typified how easily young men could move freely across the country – particularly east to west – since the railroads had radically transformed American life. Born in Indiana, Lafe Thompson attended Indiana State University and taught school for four terms. He learned the trades of a miller and printer and clerked in a general merchandise store before he read law for a short time in Goshen, Indiana. He left for Harlan in Shelby County, Iowa, where he clerked in a general

Lafayette Thompson, a Norton County attorney, served as one of the two defense lawyers for Ellen Lunney. (Photo from F. M. Lockard, *The History of the Early Settlement of Norton County, Kansas*.)

merchandise store before again studying law. In January 1878, after passing an extensive two-day examination on the law, Thompson went into practice for himself.

The lure of the unsettled west snared another young man, and in 1879 Thompson came west to Norton County. He began a law practice in partnership with M. W. Pettigrew in Norton and embarked on a career in politics, joining the main party in the Midwest in that day – the Republican party. He played the bass drum in the newly established coronet band in Norton. He dabbled in real estate, practiced law and, for a short time, moved to Pottawatomie County, Kansas, to try his luck in eastern Kansas.

But young Lafe Thompson soon moved back in Norton and

engaged in several aspects of the city's and county's public life. He formed a partnership in several endeavors with P. H. Loomis. They joined in the real estate business as well as a law practice, and together they started a newspaper, the *Norton Champion*. Thompson dropped out of publishing, selling the *Champion* to John William Conway, when elected county attorney in 1884. He practiced law with his partner, Charles D. Jones, and became the local attorney for the Chicago, Rock Island and Pacific Railroad when the Rock Island line was built to Norton in 1888. Thompson was Norton County's Republican party chairman in 1894 and had been mentioned prominently as the party's congressional candidate. He walked away from that race but decided to run for state representative. In 1894 he also had been a candidate for the Norton City Council.

One other aspect of Lafe Thompson's life: he once had been addicted to alcohol, and he freely admitted it. In the winter of 1891 he traveled to Dwight, Illinois, and took the Keeley Treatment, "graduating" from the institution there on January 18, 1892. He spoke frequently about "taking the cure" and helped others who had been battling addiction to alcohol. His reformation from his years of drinking was well known. Thompson readily told others that he was available if they needed help overcoming their dependence on alcohol.

While Jones selected a local attorney, Wilder, Thompson went out of town to find Clinton Angevine to help in the defense. It would not be long before everyone knew how important Clint Angevine would be to preparing Ellen Lunney's case.

Clinton Angevine, short and stout, looked like Napoleon with mustache and glasses. He used the colorful verbiage, the stiff English that was customary in the nineteenth century courtrooms better than almost any defense lawyer practicing in the northern part of the state where he was born and educated. The grandiloquent Angevine had been a country lawyer in Mankato, a town eighty miles east of Norton and about the same size as the Norton County seat. He literally was too good a lawyer for a small town in the middle of the Kansas plain and had moved to Kansas City, Kansas, to practice there, where he was seemed to be doing quite well. Angevine had grown out of the old school. He spoke fluently and with great feeling. His thoughts often became long spoken paragraphs, but he seemed to know when to reduce these lengthy words when he appeared before a jury.

Angevine had connected earlier with Norton County when he assisted the prosecution in a well-known murder trial in Norton in 1880. Before the Lunney rape and murder in the summer of 1894, one of the Norton newspapers, in a news item, noted that Angevine had been in Lenora. He also participated in another criminal case in Norton earlier in 1894. This only adds to the mystery of the hard-to-follow Clinton Angevine, but he clearly ranked as a fine lawyer and legal mind clearly in demand outside Jewell County where he once lived.

> *Miss Ellen Lunney, who shot and killed McEnroe, waived examination before Squire Thuma, at Lenora, on Saturday last, and was committed for trial at the September term of the district court. So also were McKeniff and the girl's brother Thomas, who are being held as accessories to the crime.*
>
> Norton Courier, *August 9, 1894.*

Six

"*The courtroom is packed to suffocation with each one craning his neck to get a glimpse of the fair defendant and to hear the proceedings. Many ladies are in attendance and seem to take much interest in it. A satisfactory jury was secured after a day and a half's labor, and shortly after the noon adjournment, the state commenced the prosecution of a case which marks an epoch in the lives of three young people – Ellen Lunney, a winsome, modest appearing young lady of eighteen summers; Thomas Lunney, a quiet harmless appearing lad of about sixteen, and John McKeniff, a man about twenty-five or thirty years old, a cousin of the other two, who are charged with murdering Eugene McEnroe, a neighbor's son, a young man well and favorably known in the community, and who had been an intimate acquaintance of the Lunney brother and sister almost from infancy.*

"*There are some ninety witnesses in the case, and at the present rate of progress, it will take the whole week and probably more to unravel the mystery which seems to surround the case.*"

Norton Courier, September 27, 1894.

"Hear ye, hear ye, the Honorable A. C. T. Geiger. All persons will rise please."

With the words of the bailiff – Clerk Dan Hart – opening the trial, Judge A. C. T. Geiger took his seat on the bench, smoothed his dark hair and asked: "Are all parties ready?"

Both sides indicated they were ready. All three defendants sat quietly and listened to Geiger prepare the courtroom that was jammed with spectators, particularly women, for the trial in the case of State of Kansas vs. Ellen Lunney, John McKeniff and Thomas Lunney.

Seated in front of Judge Geiger were Ellen Lunney, her brother, Tom, and John McKeniff, three young persons prepared for a ordeal that would change their lives. Ellen was nineteen years old, Tom seventeen and McKeniff – he was one of those who people customarily called by his last name – was age twenty-five. Towns-people jammed the court room particularly to watch the high drama of a young woman with a good reputation fight to avoid a lifetime in prison.

The trial opened in early fall, one of the more pleasant times of the year in western Kansas. By then the harsh summer heat had dis-appeared, and cold winter weather still hovered over a far horizon. Because of the large number of people crowding into the court room, it still was warm in the second-floor courtroom, and windows had been opened to allow inside what breezes would wander by.

The trial would last two weeks, even longer than the lawyers and newspapers predicted, because of the unusual lengths that the

The Norton County courtroom during the Heaton trial in 1894, a few months before Ellen Lunney's famous murder trial. Seated at left beside the table was Clinton Angevine, the Kansas City, Kansas, lawyer who built a reputation as one of the state's best criminal defense lawyers when he lived in Mankato. In the Heaton case, Angevine worked with the lawyer next to him, L. H. Wilder, but they would be on opposite sides in the Lunney case. Seated to the right of Judge C. W. Smith is believed to be Lafayette Thompson. (Photo courtesy of Kansas State Historical Society, Topeka, Kansas.)

Lunney family had taken to fight to keep their daughter and the two young men from from being convicted of murder.

Ellen could look around the large courtroom and see a space that seemed to have been built for trials with large audiences. The doors' wood paneling broke the whiteness of the stark walls, harsh and undecorated by art except for American and Kansas flags hanging from the wood window frames. Ellen, her brother and McKeniff took their seats in front of the judge and the witness chair where all eventually would sit to tell their story. Her mother sat behind her in one of the spaces reserved for the public. Ellen wore modest, store-bought long dresses that stressed her femininity. She could run her fingers along the top of the long, lacquered wooden table that served both defense and plaintiff attorneys and stretched the length of much of the area in front of the judge. She would sit and listen until called as a witness.

Several spittoons had been placed beneath the long table near where Ellen, the other defendants, their attorneys and the prosecution would sit. The men customarily wore white shirts, some with long neckties and others with bow ties on ribbons around their necks. This room had been designed for men. The women could sit in front of the heavy wooden bar that separated the public from those doing business with the court if they were charged with a crime; but except for Ellen the women in the masculine-looking room would sit only in the audience, behind the bar. Ladies did not sit on juries in 1894. The women watching would have been well aware that this was a trial of a young woman by a group of male jurors, male attorneys and a male judge.

The room had several large windows to allow air to flow into the room, which everyone knew could grow warm in the dry, early-autumn days. The open windows also allowed sounds from the street to penetrate the court room, noises from squeaky wagons pulled by large horses, their hooves digging into the soft dirt of the street. Those in the room also would have been greeted by the audible sounds of commerce arising from the downtown street businesses – screen doors closing, customers greeting friends and the high voices of young children yelling to chums or conversing with their parents. School would not open until October.

Smells would have penetrated the room and added to the lilac perfume worn by the women in the audience. Horses, sweating in the noonday sun, added their barnyard odor to the smell of fruits and vegetables that sat in front of the grocery stores that shared the street storefronts. A blacksmith's hammer occasionally banged its bass notes that clanged through the air. A soft breeze sometimes blew off the dry prairie in the morning, but by noontime it had changed to warmer puffs of air that caused women to wave their hand-held fans gently in hopes of keeping the air, the smells and the noise moving.

The audience focused mainly on one person, Ellen Lunney. She sat quietly at the defense table, a country girl sitting out of place amidst many city dwellers more cultured and alert to what happened throughout the country. The nation, and particularly Kansas, had been in political turmoil for more than two years as populists demanded economic change such as lower rail rates and higher prices for farm products. Much of the struggle added up to class warfare between a aristocracy of small town Republicans and what they termed the rabble of the plains, the populists and Democrats who had become a debtor group clamoring for change. Did Ellen feel that she was treading on the turf of those who made the rules and then changed them by allowing Gene McEnroe to remain free and terrify her after he had done terrible violence to her body? Descriptions of Ellen Lunney painted by the newspaper writers portray a young, depressed woman who felt the pressure of being prosecuted and who already showed the strain of awaiting her fate from a jury of twelve men.

She must have been terrified.

⌇

On September 27, 1894, John Conway of the *Norton Champion* described what was happening in the Norton County Courthouse.

> While the jury was being selected the three defendants were the center of all eyes, and the court room was crowded to its fullest capacity with men and women.
>
> A pen picture of the principal defendant will scarcely convey to the mind a clear notion of her looks, but there are certain strong features that may be outlined to expose her general character.
>
> About the first impression one would have by a cursory glance is her excessive modesty. She looks like one disposed to retire within herself, to withdraw from the gaze. Her face is clearly, transparently pale, but frequently colored with a blush, checkered, and quite beautiful. She has a general complexion of a healthy Irish beauty, a character of beauty that has been frequently noticed in this country, which in Europe had a historic

interest long before Lord Byron made it famous in Don Juan. Her face is long, eyes blue-gray (Irish blue) hair dark and abundant, protruding chin but delicate, upper lip slightly advanced, mouth compressed – partially bowed but conveying the impression of a powerful will and an undaunted spirit. She is over the average height, slender in build weighing perhaps 120 pounds. On a general view she would impress one as beautiful, but the unsatisfied eye will somehow turn to her again and again with disappointment because she strikes one as not being affectionate, not responsive to a heart-throb of love at the full.

The circuit-riding District Court Judge, A. C. T. Geiger, lived in Oberlin, the Decatur County seat located thirty-five miles west of Norton. Geiger, a dark-haired German, was considered a better-than-average judge. He had been born forty-six years before in Tipton, Iowa. He lived on an Iowa farm until he was nineteen years old when he entered the sub-freshman class at Carthage College at Carthage, Illinois. He stood high in his class and in his junior year received an award given for winning an oratorical contest, a skill he would use for the rest of his life. He graduated and taught school, read law, worked on the family farm and in 1885 won admittance to the Iowa Bar. A year later he moved to Oberlin, where he set up his law practice in a growing Kansas community with a shortage of lawyers. He was described as "a progressive Republican," but he campaigned for the populist Lorenzo Lewellyn in the recent governor's race. Geiger himself ran for public office in 1886 and was elected county attorney and then re-elected to a second term. When a vacancy occurred on the district court bench in 1893, he resigned his position as county prosecutor and sought and won the judgeship.

Geiger's judicial district covered several counties in Western Kansas, but Geiger apparently did not mind riding the circuit. He had a good reputation as a scholarly judge who kept up with changes in statutory and case law. Geiger had married his college sweetheart, and the two had several children who attended school in Oberlin.

The handsome Geiger had dark brown hair, a large bushy mustache and strong manly features that women considered attractive.

A. C. T. Geiger moved to Oberlin, Kansas, in 1885. A year later the voters elected him county attorney. A few years later he became a district court judge riding the circuit to handle judicial matters for several counties, including Norton County. (Photo from *Kansas, A Cyclopedia of State History,* Standard Publishing Co., 1912.)

Most of Geiger's professional friends knew him by his initials, A. C. T. Even when he died 35 years later, after a career as a prosecutor, judge, railroad attorney and and a buyer and seller of real estate, he was referred to by his initials in the obituary. For whatever reason, he declined to use his real name, Abel Cutler Tyler Geiger.

It was inevitable that local attorneys would become important players in local politics. A political career beckoned young politicians with a gift for oratory, and most lawyers saw themselves as good orators regardless of how proficient they were in persuading a crowd with their message. Besides, the local political club – and in most of small town Kansas that meant the Republican organization in the years after the Civil War – served as a social organization where the lawyers and businessmen gathered, developed friendships and maintained some control over the community's public activities.

Lafe Thompson's practice primarily had been criminal law. It was said that as a prosecutor, he had secured more convictions of criminals in proportion to the number prosecuted than any county attorney in Kansas. In addition, he felt he had a political career ahead, depending more than a little on whether the populists continued as a strong political force in Kansas. Thompson had rejected running for office as a populist, although he had been asked. He felt his political future lay with the Republican Party.

In every important criminal case tried for years in Norton County, Lafe Thomson had been involved, either as the prosecutor or a defense attorney.

Clint Angevine, when he lived in Mankato, Kansas, served three terms as county attorney, meaning that all four lawyers involved in the Lunney trial – Thompson, Jones, Wilder and Angevine – were experienced prosecutors in criminal cases. And all were roughly the same age and had prospered in the small towns of northwest Kansas.

~

Without a court reporter in the courtroom, two editor-reporters from the *Norton Courier* and *The Champion* would provide history with an account of what happened in that trial. Newspapers had been published at different times in Lenora, but none were being printed in 1894. For this trial the news emanated from the county seat of Norton.

Reporters for both newspapers used a different style of reporting than is used by most large twenty-first century American newspapers in covering trials. Today's newspapers, if they cover criminal trials, usually quote the attorney's or judge's question and the answer of the witness. The newspapers of the 1890s tried to cover all testimony on this important trial but seldom bothered to repeat the question. They focused on the answers, and then they did not report all of them, but wove those they did report into a cohesive dialogue. They did not bother to correct the grammar of the often unschooled witnesses.

The *Norton Courier* described the court room in this manner: "The court room is packed to suffocation with each one craning his neck to get a glimpse of the fair defendant and to hear the proceedings.

"Many ladies are in attendance and seem to take much interest in it," said the *Courier* in one of several observations that would be made about the unusual interest in the trial by women in the community. There was something about this case that brought in women, mainly from Norton, to watch the prosecution of this young frail defendant named Ellen Lunney.

The *Courier* had observed that Ellen Lunney was "a winsome, modest appearing young lady" and that the victim, Eugene McEnroe, was "a young man well and favorably known in the community and who had been an intimate acquaintance of the Lunney brother and sister almost from infancy."

The editor of the *Norton Champion* was J. W. Conway, who was en route to becoming one of the state's legendary editors. Upon his death in 1933, when he had published the *Champion* for forty-nine years, one of his contemporaries would comment on his seemingly unlimited vocabulary, and that his "fund of historic facts was limitless and always at his tongue's end."

Conway had earlier been the young drama critic for the Chicago Times before he was fired when an actor disagreed strongly with Conway's analysis of his performance. The actor won his fight with the Times, and a chastened John Conway left the Chicago newspaper for

J. W. Conway, the publisher of the *Norton Champion*, followed the Ellen Lunney trial. His articles remain a main source of what happened at the trial. (Photo from F. M. Lockard, *The History of the Early Settlement of Norton County, Kansas*.)

opportunities to the west. Conway's reporting on the trial was the more complete and, hence, is the most-often quoted here. Conway's politics was Republican and his support went to those from the party that represented small town businesses in the middle and northern United States. He tended to be critical of some aspects of Jones' prosecution, and Conway's comments seem to have sound basis. It might be noted that Conway had purchased his newspaper a decade earlier from Lafe Thompson, and that the attorney routinely advertised his availability as a lawyer, and his office's convenient location in the courthouse, in the *Champion*.

The *Norton Courier* was represented by Frederick Duvall, who had come to Norton from Chicago in April 1877. Although Fred Duvall had a degree in medicine, he wanted to enter business and, after operating a hardware store for several years, became the editor of the six-year-old *Courier* in 1886 and its publisher the following year. Duvall, with the help of his wife and his growing family, would publish the paper for nearly a half century. He, like most of middle America's merchants in the northern states, was a Republican, an ardent establishmentarian and small-town urban promoter who participated actively in the party politics of the time. At different times he served as a state representative and a member the local school board. This was not an editor who shied from civic duty. The community could count on Duvall being active in practically all civic organizations in Norton.

Another newspaper, the *Liberator*, a populist publication owned by D. W. Hull, covered at least some of the trial but seemed more preoccupied with reporting about the politics and economic problems of the day.

How did the trial look to those present?

"Never since the county of Norton was organized has there been a trial that has awakened the deepest interest of the people as this," said the *Norton Courier*. "From the start of the trial the courtroom has been filled to overflowing with an eager throng of men and women anxious to see and hear the proceedings. The case is being hotly and closely contested by each side even to, at times, acrimony."

Conway of the *Champion* dug deeper, even lecturing the judge and lawyers on their pronunciation:

"On the first day the regular panel and a special venire were exhausted before they were passed for cause and six or seven peremptory challenges. The court therefore continued the case until Tuesday morning to draw a further venire in the regular way by selecting from the assessors' returns rather than to complete the jury by talesmen. This was requested by the defense as the proper method," said the reporter for The *Norton Champion* who showed more interest in the jury selection than the *Courier*.

"The state allowed eighteen peremptory (a word which the court and bar persisted in pronouncing falsely by accenting the second, rather than the first, syllable against the law as found in Webster's commentaries on English words and the instructions of this paper) challenges, and the defense thirty-six peremptory challenges," said the *Champion's* J. W. Conway, who was unafraid of using his own columns to criticize or argue with attorneys or public figures.

The *Champion's* editor also proved insightful enough to comment more fully on the challenges to jurors.

> Mr. Angevine (one of the two defense attorneys) held that in no case, by statute or ruling of the Supreme Court, could the state exercise more than six challenges; the defense are allowed twice that number. As there are three defendants each one has the personal right to use twelve challenges and as they are being tried jointly (which the state could have avoided by severance if it so elected at the time of filing the complaints) the defendants are entitled to thirty-six challenges.

That was the first appearance of the problem of trying three alleged criminals on different charges in the same trial. Severance into three trials, or even two, would have been fairer but much more work for the busy prosecutor, C. D. Jones. Conway wrote:

> Mr. Wilder (one of the two prosecutors) responded that observing that the Supreme Court, and the statute as well, gave liberal construction to the singular or plural uses of words; that if the 'defendant' as used in the statute be held to mean 'defendants' under other circumstances, it will apply as well to the state. Hence if the defense is allowed thirty-six challenges, the state must be granted eighteen; otherwise the defense, if so disposed, could

pack the jury, excuse even the present twelve and twelve more besides, all this while the state (if Angevine's position is correct) must sit helplessly without remedy or resource.

The defense attorneys acted as though they were prepared to make a major issue of the composition of the jury. In the end they did not challenge many jurors.

While Norton County had an enumerated population of 9,711 in 1894 (180 fewer persons than a year earlier) only about 3,000 votes were cast during the general election in that year. This would be a large turnout of voters, indicating a society that was tuned into the political issues of the day.

Women, of course, were not counted among the number of potential voters since they were not allowed to vote except in local elections and were not permitted to sit on juries.

Also of interest to the prosecution was whether the potential jurors had read about the case in *The Champion*. "It was in the view of Colonel Jones (the other prosecutor) ample excuse to challenge for cause, a compliment well deserved," reported the *Champion*.

For whatever reason, and it could have been because of one single newspaper story in the *Champion*, jury selection did not become as contentious as it could have. By noon on Tuesday, the trial's second day, a jury had been selected from a list of fifty-two sworn local men. The defense challenged only four persons.

Those jamming themselves into the courtroom watched a jury being assembled that consisted of a panel of 12 men, to wit: G. F. Breon, C. H. Hubbard, Peter Larson, H. Whitehall, L. L. Drake, Ed Hooper, D. M. Clouse, E. G. Wilson, S. A. Winklepleck, James Palmer, Phillip Short and J. M.

Warner. Winklepleck would be chosen jury foreman.

The jurors seemed representative of the county at large. Most had English or northern European family names. The names generally are Anglo-Saxon, and one would expect that the religion of those chosen probably is closer to Protestant than Roman Catholic, the religion of the defendants and the slain young Eugene McEnroe. It would be difficult to say whether the defense found the jury it wanted. Most of the twelve veniremen lived in or near Norton, which is in the northern party of the county, and one lived near Edmond, probably twelve to fifteen miles from the Lunneys' farm in the southwestern part of the county. Regarding the age of the jurors, a majority seem from what census information is available to have been in their twenties or thirties. Most lived in rural areas.

But the remarkable fact is that none of the jurors lived near the Lunneys. None were neighbors. All those chosen lived in other parts of the county.

The prosecution in the Lunney murder trial tried to steer its case away from any mention of the rape. However, a large segment of the community seemed to have some knowledge of the event and the shooting. The jurors might have known about the happenings in the southwest part of the county if they had read the *Champion* on August 9 – most probably why Colonel C. D. Jones asked the prospective veniremen if they had read about the case in the newspaper. The story may account for why the defense decided it wanted a jury from the northern part of the county, not the south or southwest where people had made up their minds about the case. Why else would the defense accept a jury so unbalanced that no one from near Lenora sat on it?

The *Champion's* story on "The Almelo Tragedy" reported on the reaction to McEnroe's shooting in the town of Lenora.

"The writer," presumably J. W. Conway, the *Champion's* editor, "found the people in Lenora arrayed seemingly unanimously against the girl and her cousin."

This is a harsh judgment of Ellen's neighbors about her innocence. They believed she was the guilty party. The *Champion* decided the good people of Lenora didn't make their judgment based on sound information:

> The reasons for their position when searched out were not based upon their own personal knowledge, nor upon the information supplied by any person who might know the inner facts; rather, because the indefinite verdict of the community was that something was yet to be explained, some

mystery was hereafter to be resolved," said the Champion. "We were told that Tom, Dick and Harry held the opinion with good reason and information for so holding, that an innocent boy was maliciously murdered, or at least murdered as a scapegoat. When Tom, Dick and Harry were interviewed we found they held no such opinions of their own accord. We ran down every rumor to its chaotic state where it took on the form of idle dreams or vain surmises.

No one knew anything positively; suspicion, imagination, fancy, ignorance, knavery put forth their picolored theories until the brain became dizzy with contentions.

All whom we met who hold that Eugene McEnroe was innocent of the crime of rape say that they believe he was murdered deliberately in order to screen future developments limited in time from six to nine months when the guilt of John McKeniff and Ella Lunney would scandalize both.

Lenora residents seemed to believe there was a pregnancy involved and that the love-bitten John McKeniff was the father. His feelings for Ellen Lunney must not have been well hidden.

"This is the one prevailing opinion: there is no other among the maligners of the unfortunate girl," said the paper.

The *Champion* found one person who thought Ellen Lunney was confused about the rapist.

One solitary theorist held as his opinion the possibility that John McKeniff (the cousin who is thought to be deeply in love with the girl) committed the rape and that she is in error as to the identity, thus killing the wrong man. Such a theory, if proven true, would free the girl because her honesty is a justification; if there was a doubt in her mind arrayed against a dozen circumstances that McEnroe was the man, it argues an extenuation for the act.

Then the *Champion* indulged in a strange bit of prairie science about whether a rape could produce offspring.

It may be well for us here to state that in the history of the race of humanity there is not one record of a birth which is the outcome of a rape. It is a physiological impossibility to produce offspring through rape in the animal kingdom, at least among vertebrates – and it is a question with scientists if at all.

The *Champion's* opinion was that "some form of love, consent or acquiescence must solemnize procreation."

74

It's difficult to determine where the *Champion* obtained such erroneous information about rapes being incapable of producing a pregnancy. But the interpretation was clear: Should Ellen Lunney give birth in nine months, the child could not have been Eugene McEnroe's! So any child would have to have belonged to someone else – probably John McKeniff.

The newspaper article supposedly based on interviews in Lenora covered a lot of territory. It referred to Ellen as "a beautiful girl of nineteen, well bred, leaning strongly to learning, a graduate of the county system" and "a modest, retiring, studious, intellectual young woman . . . charged upon the instant of murdering an innocent neighbor to hide the guilty love between herself and an illiterate, ignorant and gawky cousin."

The article also said that Eugene McEnroe was home in bed the night of the alleged crime and that John McKeniff was "one and one half mile away on his claims."

Ellen was in the house alone, her two brothers asleep 100 yards away in the granary.

The character of the two families gained the attention of the *Champion*.

"Two neighboring families whose record of morals has not been before colored by scandal or crime are now pitted against each other forever."

The paper had a few words about the crime of rape.

"Rape is a crime with which people have indulged no patience."

What if Eugene McEnroe had committed the rape?

"If Eugene McEnroe committed the rape his death was well deserved. If innocent and known to be so by Miss Lunney, no torture conceivable even to savagery is competent to inflict just punishment in which case the cry should be, 'Upon horror's head let horrors accumulate.'"

≈

The three defendants came from a different class than the scholarly Geiger, or even most of the attorneys and officials of the court. It is unclear if either Tom Lunney or John McKeniff had attended any high school, or even what amount of grade school education they had. Living in the countryside, they probably remained quite conscious that they came from the farm and lacked what advantages there were of growing up in one of the small towns. An elementary school education was considered sufficient by many people living in rural areas. John and Anna Lunney had received little formal education, and by 1894 of the three defendants only Ellen had pursued the benefits of a high school education.

The politics of the three young defendants is not known. Were they prairie populists or Democrats, as most Irish were? Chances are they did not vote Republican, the party that held most of the offices in the towns of Kansas.

Seven

Colonel Jones opened his case against the defendants and said little about the case. He simply read the formal complaint he had filed against the three defendants:

> I, Charles D. Jones, county attorney of and for Norton County, Kansas, in the name, by the authority and on behalf of the said State of Kansas, give information and charge that on the 31st day of July, 1894, in the said county of Norton and said state of Kansas, the defendants above named, Ellen Lunney, John McKeniff and Thomas Lunney, then and there being with the wrongful, unlawful, malicious and feloniously, willfully, deliberately, premeditatedly, and on their own malice aforethought did kill and murder one Eugene McEnroe by shooting him, the said Mr. McEnroe, with a certain pistol, commonly called a revolver, then and there loaded with powder and leaden balls, which said pistol, loaded as aforesaid, the said Ellen Lunney, John McKeniff and Thomas Lunney, in their hands had and held and fired and shot said balls from the said pistol at, against, into and through the body of the said Eugene McEnroe thereby inflicting upon and through the body of he, the said Eugene McEnroe, three mortal wounds from the effects of which said mortal wounds so inflicted as aforesaid, the said Eugene McEnroe, in the said county of Norton and State of Kansas, on the said 31st day of July, 1894, instantly died, contrary to the form of the Statute in said cases made and provided and against the Peace and Dignity of the State of Kansas.

Jones confined his remarks to a simple description of the shooting of Gene McEnroe and tried to connect John McKeniff and Tom Lunney to the murder by their involvement in the purchase of the gun. By standards of the twenty-first century, the charge is sloppily drawn. It charges the two boys with the actual shooting, of which there was no evidence.

And Jones would fight to keep any mention of the rape from the trial. He would argue that the rape and murder lacked a direct connection. After all, the rape occurred a week earlier.

The colonel did not mention the penalty for murder in Kansas, but in 1894 Kansas law said it was death by hanging by the neck. But many things in Kansas were not what they seemed, and capital punishment was one of them. Albert H. Horton, president of the state bar in 1887, explained in a speech that, in reality, convicted murders were sent to the penitentiary to remain until the governor fixed the date of execution. "No execution can take place until a year has intervened after the conviction," Horton explained to the Kansas Bar Association. Then it was discretionary with the governor whether the death sentence was carried out. Custom, not statute, had imposed a one-year cooling period before the person could be hanged.

So far all of the Kansas governors had refused to assume the responsibility of ordering the death of any murderer, "no matter how atrocious or brutal his crime," Horton said. "In all these cases the counsel for the accused argue to the jury with great earnestness and seriousness that if a verdict of guilty is returned, death on the scaffold is imminent. Yet, in Kansas, there are no scaffolds erected, and such appeals are purely fanciful."

Women defendants in murder crimes seemed harder to convict than men, especially if the accused lawyers cast them as demure and ladylike. Lawyers and jurors undoubtedly remembered a murder case a year earlier in Massachusetts. Then a jury acquitted a thirty-two-year-old spinster named Lizzie Borden of killing her stepmother and father. But that didn't stop the street urchins and sensational newspapers from publicizing the jurors' verdict in a chant:

> *Lizzie Borden took an axe*
> *And gave her mother forty whacks.*
> *And when she saw what she had done*
> *She gave her father forty-one.*

Norton's merchants were in financial trouble, as the newspapers from the days of the trial tell us, when the Lunney case began in the courthouse. Norton's State Street, a strong commercial row of businesses, stood to the west of the courthouse and north of Main Street and constituted what locally was called "Banana Row." Old timers said the name originated from the tendency of store proprietors fronting nearby Kansas Avenue to throw old banana crates and other refuse out the back door, creating an unfavorable atmosphere for their competitors and an unsavory odor for others in the small town.

The men and women wanting a respite from the Lunney trial could walk to the Kahn Shoe and Clothing Company, which bought a front-page advertisement in the *Champion* newspaper to say that, because of poor crops everywhere and a rural depression, the store was offering $30,000 worth of men's "new and seasonable clothing" at "about one-third of their cost of production." Everything in the store was reduced. Ladies' jackets could be had starting at $1.00. ". . . the better goods represented this year make some of the handsomest garments used this fall ever exhibited in this country," said the advertisement. "The large sleeves and fine materials command your especial attention." Men's suits could be bought for as low as $3.75 or $5.50, depending on the quality; and fine English worsteds, clays, twills and meltons at "a discount of $9.95." Men's overcoats or ulsters cost less than $5.00 and men's boots and shoes "at what they will bring." The stores obviously suffered from the Panic of '93 and hoped advertising would help them attract what few customers were buying new clothes.

The Norton Mercantile Co., perhaps advertising in anticipation that the trial would bring in new customers, also placed much of its merchandise on sale. "We must close out . . . our immense stock of dry goods, boots and shoots, hats and caps," said a newspaper advertisement.

Other merchants, probably hurting badly from the severe depression by this point in the early days of autumn, advertised frequently in both newspapers.

The economic news dominated the news columns. Each new

copy of the weekly newspapers carried lists of land foreclosures in Norton County. The land, said the notices, would be sold at a future date on the courthouse steps by Sheriff George R. Betterton. In a busy week, it was not unusual for Betterton to sell a half dozen farms or properties foreclosed because the occupying family couldn't meet their bills.

$\sim$

As Anna Lunney watched the trial, she must have wondered how the Lunney family could raise the cash necessary to pay the defense lawyers. Questions about the Lunney family's financial situation have remained unanswered as no documents have been uncovered to reveal how they paid for their extraordinary legal costs in 1894. With a lack of cash, they could have borrowed to raise the money. John and Anna Lunney, with substantial land ownership, might well be "good for it" as the saying goes, without having cash to pay pending bills.

Anna Lunney certainly attended the week-long trial, as she would be called as a witness, but it is not clear whether John Lunney did. The defense attorneys would steer from calling the Lunney father apparently because of something he said or may have said at the scene of the shooting.

Since the prosecution did not call him as a witness either, it is unclear whether he was present. John Lunney apparently was tending to his horses when the shooting at the school occurred, but it remains surprising that John Lunney would not be called to discuss events in the week between the rape and shooting.

$\sim$

"Mr. Jones, are you prepared to call your first witness?" the prosecution was asked.

"We are, your honor," said C. D. Jones.

It would be the job of the Colonel to show what happened at Thuma School, describing the events through witnesses to show that Ellen Lunney killed Eugene McEnroe in cold blood. In 1894 court procedures had not been defined as rigidly as they would be in the twentieth century, and the result would be witnesses coming to testify several times in the trial. If attorneys on one side forgot to ask an important question, they simply would ask the witness, if he or she still were in the neighborhood, to come back and clear up the matter.

The prosecution summoned its first witness, J. P. Bozarth, but quickly excused him temporarily when told that Mrs. Catherine Peak was ready to testify and that her father had died recently and was lying at home awaiting burial in Lenora. Then, before Mrs. Peak could testify, the defense called for the exclusion of all relatives of Eugene McEnroe, except the complaining witness, James McEnroe, father of the deceased, who was described by the *Champion* as "a white-haired old gentleman who sat by with a mournful countenance." The McEnroe relatives left the courtroom. Excluding witnesses was not unusual, particularly if they would later be called to testify. Let's not give the witnesses an opportunity to coordinate their stories. No such motion was made about the Lunney kin, suggesting that except for Anna Lunney, the rest of the family, including the father, had stayed home. Of course, Ellen, son Tom and McKeniff – almost part of the Lunney family – were in court, in front of the bar, courtesy of the state. Tom and McKeniff still were lodged in jail, and Ellen stayed at Sheriff Betterton's home.

Thus began the testimony of the witnesses. Some of it was contradictory. Much seemed repetitive, but what is printed here is to show what happened from the perspective of different persons.

The testimony also indicated people came from miles away to watch what happened in the hearing, and that they had gathered in the one-room school long before the event was to begin. The residents of the countryside treated the hearing as a reason to meet, exchange news and learn what others knew but they didn't.

~

Mrs. Catherine Peak, one of the Lenora area's pioneering women, took the witness chair. She said she had lived near Lenora for twenty-one years and was acquainted with the defendants, Ellen Lunney, Tom Lunney and John McKeniff. The wife of Sol Peak, a old buffalo hunter and trapper, Catherine would have arrived in the Lenora community at approximately the same time as John Lunney and the Dunlap families.

"I have known McKeniff about six years," she said, pointing to where the defendant was sitting in the courtroom.

Most everyone, it seemed, referred to the young Irish-born man by the single name of "McKeniff."

Mrs. Peak said she wasn't personally acquainted with Eugene McEnroe but had seen him at the Thuma School House on the day of the shooting. She also saw Ellen Lunney, Mrs. John Lunney, John McKeniff and Tom Lunney at the school.

"I saw Mrs. Lunney and Ellen when they first came to the school house," Mrs. Peak said. "They came in side by side, and I saw Ellen shoot Eugene McEnroe. Eugene was sitting in a seat next to the center aisle of the school house, four, five or six feet from the door,"said Mrs. Peak.

"She shot with a revolver. Shot him in the back somewhere," saying she could not tell exactly where. "Ellen had on a long cape, and from under it she drew a revolver. I don't know how many times she shot, but three or four times for sure."

Mrs. Peak couldn't say what McEnroe or Ellen did after the shooting.

"She was in the wagon or buggy the next time I saw her," Mrs. Peak said. "She was sitting there with her mother. It was a light spring wagon. I next saw Eugene McEnroe being carried into the school.

"He died in a few minutes after being laid down."

Cross examination elicited additional information.

Mrs. Peak was in the school house about a half an hour before Ellen arrived. She was part of the large crowd that had been attracted for one main reason – curiosity – although many of the witnesses phrased it differently.

"I went there out of respect for the family as they were in deep grief," she said. She also supplied some observations about McEnroe's movements, which appear to have been unrestricted.

"A few moments before the Lunneys came, Eugene got up and

moved several times. It was in plain view. I did not notice him after the Lunneys came in," she said.

"My attention was attracted to her."

The testimony of Catherine Peak set the stage for the prosecution's case: Ellen Lunney, the demure, quiet young defendant, had drawn a six-shooter from beneath her cape and sent a volley of angry shots at Gene McEnroe.

~

Next came J. P. Bozarth, who for fifteen years lived between Lenora and Clayton. "It's nine miles from Lenora where I live. I know the Thuma School House. I live six miles from it."

Bozarth did not know the defendants well and only knew Eugene McEnroe "by sight for several years." He had known Ellen when she was younger, a child. Bozarth apparently was attracted to the Thuma School House, a six-mile ride, out of curiosity from what he had heard about the case. Bozarth is listed in records in Lenora as a member of Lenora's Christian Church, but from the neighborhood in which he lived, many of the neighboring farm families most likely would have been Catholic. Bozarth testified:

> I saw Eugene, Ellen, Tom and McKeniff there. I think Eugene was in the school house when I got there. The first I saw him was in a seat opposite me. I saw Ellen and Mrs. Lunney come in the door and walk up the aisle. I next heard the shooting. I was about ten feet from it.
>
> McEnroe was sitting facing west, with his elbow resting on the seat talking to a gentleman in the next seat. I can't say how many shots were fired. They came in such quick succession. She shot with a revolver. Eugene was sitting with his back to her.

Ellen made sure she did not miss.

> She placed the pistol within a few inches of him. Eugene raised up and commenced making off. I saw him go outdoors. I didn't see him again until he was brought in.
>
> I saw the revolver taken away from Ellen by George Miller. Miller, Muzzy and Regester were there. I couldn't say what Ellen did then. I saw McKeniff and John Lunney on the outside of the house. I thought she was very composed for a lady under the circumstances. She did not seem much excited over it.

Bozarth was the first witness to comment on Ellen's coolness, her detachment from the havoc she caused in front of her.

> When brought in, Eugene was, you might say, dead. He breathed but twice after brought in.
> I could not say what was said. Everyone was excited. Eugene was laid on a long seat. After the doctor was brought in, he was laid on the floor.
> Ellen was taken back into the school house about a half hour after Eugene was taken in.

Cross examination elicited the name of the person with whom McEnroe was talking when Ellen added four, or perhaps five, lead bullets to his body.

"He was sitting with his left shoulder to the aisle talking to John Hay, who sat in the next seat behind him when the shots were fired," said Bozarth.

~

John Hay, twenty-five years old, the same age as Eugene, lived in Lenora township for about eleven years. He said that Eugene McEnroe sat beside Patsey, a brother, in the next to the last row. Witnesses, including himself, sat in the back row behind them. He saw Ellen and her mother enter through the door, glance around as if looking for a seat, then walk up the aisle, Ellen on her mother's arm.

When Ellen reached Eugene McEnroe, she pulled the revolver from beneath the long cape she was wearing and held the pistol six inches from McEnroe's shoulder.

Ellen shot five times, Hay said. Other witnesses would say four times, or three times. Hay said he saw three balls "taken out" of Gene's body. The balls entered the small of the back and the shoulder. After the shooting, a doctor took the balls from the breast and one from the groin.

Hay said "the deceased" tried to get away when the shooting commenced. Eugene McEnroe ran to the door without saying a word.

> The firing was rapid. Bob Regester tried to get the revolver from her, George Miller helping him, all struggling – she refusing to give it up.

Then Patsey McEnroe tried to get the revolver from Ellen. Tom Lunney tried to push him away. Finally Regester twisted the revolver out of her hand.

After the revolver was taken Ellen went out to the wagon, McKeniff hurrying her along.

Hay added that he did not hear McKeniff utter a word.

On cross examination by Angevine, Hay said he went to the school house at nine o'clock in the morning "with a lot of others" and was there an hour before Ellen Lunney arrived. He spent about fifteen minutes talking to Eugene McEnroe. He saw Ellen enter with her mother. Neither Tom Lunney or John McKeniff were present when Ellen and her mother arrived.

"They (Ellen and her mother) partly walked and ran to the wagon," Hay said. "About fifty people were present. McKeniff, Ellen and her mother got into the wagon while the father, John Lunney, was untying the team. They came in a lumber wagon and drove a team of black horses, each would weigh ten or eleven hundred pounds. Ellen was in the spring seat."

Other testimony would indicate that Ellen and her mother sat in the wagon but made no attempt to leave, and that confusion prevailed in and around the rural school house after the shooting.

∼

Next on the witness stand was a neighbor of the Lunneys, Arthur Taylor, who was twenty-five years old. He testified:

> I live six miles southwest of Lenora. I have lived there sixteen years. I am acquainted with the Lunneys. I know Ellen. I've known her for about ten years. I've known John McKeniff five years and Thomas Lunney about ten years. I have known Gene McEnroe eight or nine years. I saw Gene about ten o'clock in the morning on July thirty-first last," said Taylor, recalling the day of the shooting.
>
> Thomas or McKeniff were not present at the time. Later, before the shooting, they walked forward and witnesses thought they were going to take a seat.
>
> I did not see more until the first shot was fired. I saw her shoot 'the deceased.' She shot five times in succession, in rapid succession. Gene got out of the west side of the seat and ran outside.
>
> She was tolerably cool, I guess. As far as I could tell she was cool. When

she got through, the revolver was taken from her, George Miller holding her hands while Register secured it. I didn't see McKeniff. It was probably five minutes after the shooting before they reached the wagon.

I saw Tom Lunney standing back to the door. Tom ran up and pulled Patsey McEnroe away from Ellen. She went out to the wagon at a fast walk or run. McKeniff had hold of her arm. They went out to the spring wagon.

When he first saw McEnroe, he was "lying on the ground, alive, outside the school house. He was picked up and taken into the room."

Where was the buggy?

"Four or five rods from the house."

A rod is five and a half yards.

On cross examination by Angevine, Taylor said McKeniff came to the school before Ellen and her mother. Taylor also described the team of horses again. He said the team was black, and the horses pulled "a light spring wagon."

The team of paired black horses and the so-called spring wagon became an unwanted issue for the defendants. Such a team implied wealth for the Lunneys, which the defense attorneys did not want displayed. The nation had fallen into economic stagnation and political turmoil, and pointing to a what might be perceived as a display of wealth on the Lunney homestead sent the wrong message to the jury.

Eight

Slowly and deliberately the prosecution laid its groundwork. So far the two lawyers had described the scene of the murder, the Thuma school, without specifying the intention of the gathering. Colonel Jones and prosecutor Wilder had succeeded in showing Ellen Lunney as the killer of Eugene McEnroe. The two young men, Tom Lunney and John McKeniff, were being portrayed as accessories. The prosecutors hinted that the whole Lunney family may have been aware that Ellen carried a pistol under her cape and planned to use it to kill twenty-six-year-old Gene McEnroe.

Now the time had come to bring individual members of the McEnroe family to the witness stand.

The bailiff called Patsey H. McEnroe, age fifteen, to the witness chair. The U. S. Census listed the boy's name as Patrick, but everyone seemed to know him as "Patsey." Young Patsey was slim, a bit short for his age but, like his brother, Eugene, a bit of a bulldog who didn't back down from a boxing or a wrestling match. The jury would learn that Patsey also didn't mind attacking the character of Ellen Lunney if he thought it would help his brother Gene.

On the morning of July 31, Patsey, his father, brothers and a sister went to the residence of Squire Thuma. The Lunneys and McKeniff came soon after. They all went from the Squire's home to the Thuma School House. Patsey testified:

> I went to the Thuma School House about eight in the morning.
> Eugene was in the school house sitting down. I was sitting behind Eugene when the shooting began.
> I threw my arms around Ellen and grasped her arms at the waist to prevent her from shooting any more. Tom came up and caught hold of me, saying "God damn you! Let her alone!" We scuffled along the aisle to the

door when he struck me in the face. I saw Bob Regester catch Ellen's arm and try to get the revolver. Miller pried her hand open and took it from her.

Patsey would have been appalled at the Lunneys' course of action – filing a rape charge against his big brother, his idol, his hero. He had to watch while Ellen shot Eugene in cold blood in the school. And Tom, his friend for all these years! Why, a week before the shooting, Tom had gone with him to get apples from a neighbor's orchard. Tom grabbing him after he went to try to help his brother.

The prosecution asked about Ellen's mental condition.

"I don't know what her mental condition was at the time," he said. He was more interested in describing the death of his older brother. That was the issue. Not how Ellen felt after shooting his brother.

"I then ran out to see Eugene. He was in Hay's arms dying. I don't know how long he lived. They carried him into the school house."

On cross examination by Angevine, Patsey said he had been at the school house about 15 minutes before going inside. The shooting occurred about nine o'clock.

"Dan went in with me," Patsey said referring to his brother. They sat with Hay behind Eugene. About ten minutes later Ellen entered with her mother. He did not see John McKeniff or Tom Lunney in the room. Patsey did not know how many shots were fired. He thought at first there were three shots. The shots were fired in about five seconds. Ellen did not fire the gun after he grabbed hold of her wrists, Patsey said.

The prosecution, apparently hearing enough about Patsy's information about the day of the shooting, asked about events prior the his brother's death.

The questioning found that Patsey had heard shooting – two shots – exactly a week before the school house shooting. These shots were fired at two o'clock in the morning. The shots came from the direction of the Lunney farm or the nearby farm of Barney Hickert. The shots must have been fired by Tom warning the intruder not to return to the Lunney farmyard.

Patsey also commented that he had talked to his father "on the night the rape was committed."

The rape!

It was the first mention in the courtroom of a rape, an outrage in the night that the state's lawyers did not want to discuss. The prosecution had carefully steered the testimony to focus on the shooting in the rural school house but could not keep the subject out of the courtroom. Keeping the rape out of the trial would prove difficult. Here a young prosecution witness opened the door a crack.

Patsey said he didn't know why he thought it was two o'clock that he heard shooting. He was in bed at home. He did not look at a clock.

Questioning returned to the school house shooting. Patsey said that Ellen Lunney, after she left the school, never spoke a word until she got into the buggy.

~

Another of Eugene's brothers, Daniel McEnroe, eighteen years old, was the next witness called by the prosecution. Dan, like Patsey, was dressed in simple farm dress of a rough shirt and pants, possibly reflecting an attempt by the prosecution to show the McEnroe brothers as "poor but honest" youth. Dan commented on the team of horses, the black team that was becoming a representation of the wealth of the Lunney family.

"There were a good many there when I arrived. Some I knew. Some I didn't," said Dan.

He saw Ellen enter the school house "just a couple of minutes after McKeniff went out." He first saw McKeniff in front of the school. "He came inside and looked around as if he was looking for somebody." On the motion of the defense, the last seven words were stricken as a conclusion by Dan.

The witness said Ellen fired five shots. His brother Gene got out of his seat and ran outside. Dan also ran outside "to where Gene was lying on the ground.

"I suppose he was dead," Dan said of his brother.

Like Patsey, Dan had witnessed the trauma of watching his older brother being shot down in front of him. The Lunneys no longer were friends. They killed his brother. Dan must have worked hard to hide the anger that must have cried to come out.

Dan saw Ellen in the light wagon with her mother. He said Ellen "looked a little pale."

The *Norton Courier* said the cross-examination "brought out nothing new," but a review of the *Norton Champion* news columns found some testimony of interest.

The McEnroes answered, said the *Champion*, that Ellen appeared natural but very pale.

Dan also did not notice what his brother Eugene did when Ellen entered the room. This time he "noticed Ellen's unusual paleness" when she entered the door.

"Mrs. Lunney had hold of Ellen's arm in the aisle."

"Ellen looked around over the house on entering."

"She wore a black straw hat, not a sun bonnet." The prosecution had suggested she wore a sun bonnet, common on the country farms.

Presumably, a black straw hat had a dressier look than the common sun bonnet, worn by women workers in the hot, summer fields.

~

The next day, Wednesday, E. J. Muzzy, the thirty-four–year–old constable of Lenora township, was the first witness called. Muzzy, more articulate than most of the previous people called to testify, must have been a persuasive witness for the prosecution. Muzzy and E. J. Darnell were the only full-time constables at the school when the shooting occurred.

Muzzy named a dozen or more persons present at the school. Ellen and her mother arrived about fifteen or twenty minutes after Muzzy did.

Muzzy described how McKeniff stepped inside the school, took off his hat and then went outside again. He said Ellen and her mother "came in and hesitated a little as if looking for a seat.

> She appeared to be cool.
> They passed by where Gene was sitting. She stopped and took a revolver from under her cloak and shot Gene.

They walked up slow and deliberately. The mother was on the right hand side of Ellen. The mother seemingly let loose of her arm and stepped back. The shots were very quick. Gene turned his head around at the second shot then started to run out. Ellen was holding the gun right at him.

"Cool and deliberate she held the revolver in her hand and started to go away" before being disarmed, he said.

If Ellen's mother let loose of her arm, was it to allow her daughter to draw her pistol and shoot McEnroe? This represented the prosecution's view of the case. The fact that the state started to charge Mrs. Lunney but then backed away indicated the Colonel did not think he could prove such a charge. But from Muzzy's testimony, the jury should have understood that the motherly release of her daughter may have been part of a family agreement to allow Ellen to kill Gene McEnroe.

Muzzy said that McKeniff told Ellen, "Come on, come on, my dear girl, I will stand by you." They hurried to the buggy, Muzzy said, according to the *Norton Champion*. The *Norton Courier* reported that McKeniff said only, "Come my dear girl, I'll stand by you."

Muzzy also recounted a conversation he had with McKeniff on Thursday before the killing.

"He (McKeniff) wanted to know what had become of Gene McEnroe at the time he was arrested for rape," Muzzy recalled.

Again, mention of the rape. At this point, did anyone in the courthouse not know that Ellen had been raped? But nothing more was added. Gene, of course, had been released on Gabe Dunlap's bond.

On cross examination by Angevine, Muzzy said that when he arrived, Tom Lunney was present at the school house. Then the Lunneys – John, Ellen and Mrs. Lunney – arrived. McKeniff drove up in a wagon with two others. "He stood up behind the two in a seat."

Muzzy said he couldn't describe the team and didn't know if it was a "farm wagon or a spring wagon."

The general definition of a spring wagon is one whose bed is set on springs. A spring wagon is for transporting passengers. Some wagons were covered but the Lunney's wagon was not, at least not in the surviving photograph of the wagon loaded with Lunney children and their parents. Farm wagons generally were utility wagons. Usually they had no springs and often no seat. They often consisted of little more than a rectangular box bed for hauling. The driver usually stood or sat on a board seat in the front of the wagon. If a seat or a board had been provided, he and a passenger could use it as a seat. But it still would be a rougher ride than if the seat rested on springs.

John and Anna Lunney and Ellen all sat on one seat, Muzzy said. He didn't notice if Ellen was flushed or pale.

After the shooting and the scuffle over the gun, Muzzy next saw Ellen sitting with her mother in the wagon. McKeniff stood beside them. They made no effort to escape, Muzzy said.

～

Next to sit in the witness chair was Robert Regester, forty-eight years old, a well-known and respected resident of Lenora township and a Norton County resident for fifteen years.

"Ellen was perfectly cool," said Regester. He thought four shots were fired "as rapidly as she could work her finger. She seemed to be cool about it as if she intended to commit the deed."

Regester said he made several efforts to "twist the revolver from her, but did not succeed until George Miller helped by opening her fingers. McKeniff had his arms around her to pull her away. She looked back, struggling, to see who had hold of her. Patsey grabbed her before the last shot was fired, putting both his arms around her and her arms."

Regester said he did not know if he could recognize the revolver from any other of the same make. He gave it to Constable Darnell. Regester then identified the revolver offered by the prosecution, "marked 'W' on the handle, double action, five shot, caliber 38."

Cross examined by Angevine, Regester described himself as "ordinary strong," but alone he was unable to free the revolver from Ellen's grip.

"She held it with one hand," he said.

～

Elijah H. Darnell, age forty-nine, next came to the witness stand. He had been constable in Lenora township for twelve years. That Lenora, a small frontier town of more than 200 people, had two constables (Muzzy and Darnell) to maintain law and order indicates the quiet-appearing village may have had a wilder aspect than was described in local news accounts and in local histories. Because of its sizeable hinterland, Lenora always attracted people from a large area. One had to travel more than twenty miles in any direction before finding a larger town than Lenora.

Darnell said he wasn't in the school house when the shooting occurred. He walked up to the buggy where Mrs. Lunney and her daughter sat. McKeniff was in front and to the right of the team.

"With my right hand I took hold of the team. McKeniff said he would take charge of the team. I think I told him he was under arrest. When I thought he was getting the best of it, I pulled my six-shooter. Mr. Lunney said, 'Boys, he is only doing what the law requires.' Mac dropped the rope," said Darnell.

He identified the revolver, which he said he had received from Regester, "and I kept it until I turned the girl over to the sheriff."

On cross examination by Angevine, Darnell appeared less polite. Darnell said he "told McKeniff not to move or I would kill him."

He drew the revolver, Darnell said, because he saw Gabe Dunlap (uncle of Ellen Lunney, husband of Eugene McEnroe's sister and underwriter of Eugene's bail) "and I thought it was best to prepare for self defense."

Why did Darnell believe that it was best to prepare for self defense? The answer is unclear. "He did not like to give the reason," was all the *Champion* reported. For whatever reason neither the prosecution nor defense cared to pry the answer from Elijah H. Darnell.

∾

Sheriff Betterton was called to identify the revolver, but an objection was made and sustained because his name did not appear in the information given the defense.

A Lunney neighbor, Abraham Hendricks, testified that at the

time of the shooting he stood outside the school house at the north end. He saw Eugene McEnroe come out of the door, run around towards the southwest corner but fall forward, landing on his left side.

"Joel Hay went to him and turned him so I could see the face. Death was in the face. He was about dead," Hendricks said.

McEnroe was taken back inside the school. Hendricks said he saw Ellen and McKeniff hurry to the wagon. Ellen got in the wagon. McKeniff went to untie the horses.

On cross examination by Angevine, Hendricks said he went toward the wagon and inquired, "Who killed that boy?"

No one answered. Then someone said that Ellen Lunney had shot McEnroe.

"That girl don't realize what she has done," Hendricks said he replied. "This girl doesn't know what she is doing."

Before Hendricks' statements were clarified, the state moved to strike the statements, saying it was not part of the case.

"A lively discussion followed between Angevine and Wilder as to the legal admittance of this part of the testimony," reported the *Champion*. Judge Geiger sustained the motion and the words were stricken.

The argument, of course, goes to the heart of the case. Was Ellen temporarily insane at the time of the shooting? She showed unusual strength in possessing the gun and refusing to allow herself to be disarmed. She acted strangely, several witnesses said. However, Judge Geiger would have been in error to allow another person to say that Ellen did not know what she was doing. That was for lawyers to argue and for jurors to decide.

∼

Testifying next was Joel E. Hay, who said he picked up the almost lifeless McEnroe after he fell outside the school.

"I held his head on my knee until he was taken into the school house about dead. He breathed three times after being taken in, then died," said Hay, who was not cross examined. His testimony closed temporarily what had happened at Thuma school. Next

would come information about how Ellen obtained a revolver in
the first place

~

Floyd F. Richmond, who had clerked in Leonard's Hardware
Store for nine years, was called. The store's owner, Patrick Leonard,
came to the United States from County Meath, Ireland, in time to
serve a few months for the north in the Civil War, then became an
Indian fighter for the U. S. Cavalry. He received the United States
Medal of Honor for heroism for saving two women settlers and a
ten-year-old child in a battle with Cheyennes and Pawnees in 1879
in Nebraska. Then Leonard moved to growing Lenora and opened
his hardware store.

Richmond was alone in the hardware store on July 26, when
Thomas Lunney and John McKeniff came in to buy a revolver. He
identified the revolver taken from the scene of the shooting as the
"same kind" purchased by McKeniff but could not say that it was
the same one.

"It looks the same," Richmond said.

He also said that McKeniff did not say why he was buying the
revolver.

Angevine, on cross examination, elicited additional details.
Richmond said that McKeniff at the same time ordered a caster for
a lister, a farm implement used for plowing and planting. While in
the back room, McKeniff asked the price of the revolver. No other
customers were in the store. McKeniff was in the hardware store
for thirty minutes. After paying for one revolver, he decided to
exchange it for a second pistol. After McKeniff again paid for the
revolver, both men left.

The *Norton Champion* reported that the defense tried to prove
that the first thing McKeniff and Tom Lunney asked about was the
piece of machinery and after ordering it, bought the revolver.

"The witness got very mixed up," reported the newspaper. However, the testimony probably was sufficient for the prosecution
because it resulted in the weapon being identified. The revolver was
placed in evidence.

~

Dr. M. W. Drown was called, and he described Eugene McEnroe's wounds during questioning by Ledru H. Wilder. This was the first witness in which Wilder took the lead. Colonel Jones had examined all previous witnesses. Drown said he had practiced medicine in Lenora for five years. He was summoned to the school and found that four bullets had penetrated McEnroe's body. One ball apparently still was in his body.

"That's all the bullets I know of," Drown testified. It was his opinion that one ball that cut into or through the base of the heart caused the death of Eugene McEnroe.

Three of the balls were offered in evidence. Were there other bullets, or balls? No one reported finding them but other witnesses said they heard five shots. Was one still lodged in or under the school's floor? That seems most likely. No one apparently made a search to find another ball.

Under cross examination by Angevine, the doctor explained that the pulmonary artery branches about two inches from the heart, although the distance varies depending on the size of the person. McEnroe was about 135 pounds, which the doctor said was medium size, but he was slim. The pulmonary artery was severed. The effect of the severing would cause internal hemorrhaging. Angevine asked if severing the pulmonary artery would still allow Eugene McEnroe to go out the door.

Perhaps, said the doctor. However, if the aorta were severed, it would have caused instantaneous death.

~

James McEnroe, the elderly father of Gene, was in Thuma School when the shooting occurred, was summoned. He identified the coat and vest and said both were in his valise since the shooting. This time both were offered and accepted in evidence. The father as well as other members of the family would be called again.

~

William McCready, who lived in Graham County several miles south of Thuma School, said he was at the school the day of the shooting. He saw Ellen and McKeniff run to the wagon and heard McKeniff say, "Come on, come on, my dear girl, I'll stay with you till hell freezes over."

On cross examination, McCready said he was about twenty-five feet from McKeniff when the statement was made.

"John had his hand on Ellen's left shoulder, pushing her along," he said.

~

Irvin Green of Lenora also testified he heard McKeniff say, "Come on, come on, my dear girl, I will stay by you until hell freezes over."

Cross examined, Green said he approached McEnroe when he fell outside the school and was twenty feet from Ellen and John McKeniff when he heard the words spoken.

~

Effie Norlin, the young Lenora girl who had been staying at Sheriff Betterton's house, said she had talked to Ellen Lunney, who said that if "she had it to do over, she would do it again."

The testimony would have been a disappointing blow to Ellen. The two young women, nearly the same age, had lived under the same roof and probably shared secrets in their days together. Ellen must have felt betrayed. How could Effie be testifying for the prosecution?

Effie's testimony would have been a problem for Anna Lunney, Lafe Thompson and Clinton Angevine. Ellen would be asked later about Effie Norlin's testimony.

On cross examination Angevine tried to put a better face on the relationship. Under Angevine's questioning, Effie said she talked to Elijah Darnell, the Lenora constable, about the case a few days ago and never told Darnell that Ellen had told her anything about the case.

Was it unusual to lodge Ellen at the sheriff's home rather than behind bars? Perhaps, but one can only speculate about her jailing since the newspapers did not report any testimony on the question. The Betterton's home had become the depository for persons that

George Betterton became Norton County sheriff in 1893. After her arrest, Ellen Lunney would stay in Betterton's home because no jail facilities existed to house women prisoners for lengthy periods. (Photo from F. M. Lockard, *The History of the Early Settlement of Norton County, Kansas.*)

the authorities wanted held for one reason or another but not jailed.

Effie, in fact, was not charged with any crime but was being held in protective custody.

~

Seywood Larrick, the prominent Lenora banker, testified that he talked with John McKeniff about his buying a revolver in the days before the shooting. Larrick advised him to take the gun back to the store because something might happen to the McEnroes and he, McKeniff, would be held responsible for it.

"McKeniff said he was not buying it for himself," Larrick said.

Larrick, although he did not arrive in the first wave of settlement, soon became one of Lenora's early rainmakers. He and Guy Barbo built large Victorian mansions east of the downtown, two of the largest homes in town. As a banker during Lenora's hard times, Larrick picked up large tracts of valuable land across the countryside because he and his financial institution held mortgages on much of the property.

Local residents relied on his bank, which the respected Larrick kept afloat in the 1890s while other institutions closed their doors. He later built a city park with a grandstand, open areas and athletic fields that he left to a thankful community. Annual celebrations would be held in Larrick Park as long as the community needed and used it.

~

James McEnroe, father of Eugene, was recalled. He said that before the shooting of his son he heard shooting in the direction of the Lunneys on two different evenings while he was in bed. The time between the shots varied, sometimes two or three shots occurred in quick succession. His bedroom was on the east side of the house where there was one window and two doors.

On cross examination, James McEnroe said he lived in a house that was part sod and part stone. He heard shooting in the daytime and the same night about three or four days before Eugene was killed. It was either Friday or Saturday before the shooting. He heard two shots that night about ten o'clock. The following night he heard three or four shots about ten o'clock. Willie Lunney shoots rabbits "a great deal," McEnroe said. He could hear the shots because the nights were warm and the doors and windows were open. Still, McEnroe said he placed no importance on the shots and never talked to his family about the matter.

One wonders if it were that simple for James McEnroe. Was he frightened when he heard the shots? Was the shooting a warning that the Lunneys were ready to come across the river to even things with the McEnroe clan? One suspects James McEnroe may have placed considerable importance on the shots in the night and, if he had locks on his doors, may have secured them.

~

Robert Regester was recalled. Regester said he saw John Lunney inside the door when he got the revolver in his hand and heard him say, "She's done her work. She's done her work."

Angevine cross examined Regester, who said he didn't believe that John Lunney was in the school at that point. Did he have the

witnesses confused with someone else? Regester said he understood the name of the person talking was John McKeniff, not John
Lunney. Angevine moved to strike the statement as not competent.
After a debate, Judge Geiger struck the statement from evidence
that the jury would consider. Had the statement been tied directly
to John Lunney, and had anyone else heard it, the result would have
been extremely damaging to Ellen's defense.

The prosecution rested its case. The two prosecutors clearly had
demonstrated that Ellen Lunney walked into Thuma School,
pulled a revolver from beneath her cape and shot Eugene McEnroe four or five times. From the prosecutors' view, there seemed to
be no question but that the killing was premeditated. One bullet
entered the heart, but the victim still managed to run through the
school door and into the schoolyard. He died quickly. Patsey
McEnroe grabbed Ellen, and two adult men pried the gun from
her fingers.

Ellen was cool, pale and somewhat detached from the activities
at Thuma school. She was taken to the Lunney's wagon by John
McKeniff, who said something like, "Come on, my dear girl. I will
stay with you till hell freezes over." She remained at the wagon with
her parents until a constable arrested her, Mrs. Lunney and brother
Tom and friend John McKeniff. Charges were soon dropped
against Mrs. Lunney but not the two young men.

The prosecution also elicited testimony that it was McKeniff,
accompanied by Tom Lunney, who purchased the gun at the hardware store. McKeniff later told banker Larrick that he did not buy
the gun for himself. None of the lawyers pursued the question
about why McKeniff purchased the gun because McKeniff and
Tom Lunney had not been on the witness stand. They still were
charged in the same indictment as Ellen.

Was John McKeniff in love with Ellen, and would that information come forth for the jury to hear? Why did McKeniff buy the
pistol, or did Tom make the actual purchase or the selection? Did
Ellen tell McKeniff or Tom to buy the revolver so she could kill
Eugene McEnroe?

And did the Lunney family conspire to kill Eugene McEnroe by obtaining the pistol for her and then turning their backs while Ellen walked up behind Gene and shot him? That was the prosecution's explanation of the murder of Eugene McEnroe, and at this point the jury may have believed that was exactly what happened.

Nine

At the same time the Lunney trial was in the news, another rape had caught the attention of Lenora and Norton County citizens. A sixty-one-year-old physician in Lenora, J. M. S. Thomas, was charged with raping Effie Norlin, the young Lenora girl. Her family had brought the charges. Effie was eighteen years old, but the doctor's relationship and intercourse with her apparently had begun years earlier.

Dr. Thomas and his wife had provided a home for Effie Norlin for several years, and the doctor supposedly had sexual relations with her since she was age thirteen. The girl told a married sister about the relationship in the spring of 1894.

"When he (Thomas) was confronted by the girl's relatives, the doctor skipped town. He was arrested in Nebraska and now here awaits sentence," the *Champion* told its readers on September 27, three days after the start of the Lunney trial.

Judge Geiger and a jury – a different one than the men selected to hear the Lunney case – heard the Thomas case on September 18. Colonel Jones prosecuted, and attorneys J. R. Hamilton and Lafe Thompson represented Thomas. The jury, after two hours deliberation, convicted the aging doctor of rape.

Two weeks later, during a recess in the Lunney trial, Thomas asked for a new trial, which Geiger refused. Geiger, on October 5, then sentenced Thomas to five years hard labor in the Kansas State Penitentiary.

The sentence of five years hard labor probably killed Thomas. Records indicate he died in 1898, four years into his sentence.

Kansas penal life proved harsh for prisoners, and many died

before finishing their sentences. One Kansan told his story of how horrific penal life could be. John N. Reynolds, an Atchison, Kansas, publisher of a small newspaper, became involved in a political fight in which he supported the wrong candidate for district judge. He managed to get himself indicted for using the mail for fraudulent purposes and received a sentence of eighteen months in the penitentiary at Lansing, Kansas, a term that Reynolds called "political spite" for fighting an entrenched local ring in Atchison.

He wrote a book, "Hell In Kansas or Life in the Kansas Penitentiary" in which he described his prison life and his job for his first six months: digging in the prison's coal mines.

"The young, the old, the middle-aged are indiscriminatory and unceremoniously thrust into the mine. Down there are nearly five hundred prisoners. Among them are boys from seventeen to twenty years of age, many of whom are in delicate health. Here are found old men, some sixty years of age," said Reynolds. He told the story of George Lennox, a stealer of horses serving his second prison term.

> Sedgwick County sent him to the prison the first time for a similar offense. During the winter of 1887 and 1888 he worked in the coal mines. The place where he was laboring seemed dangerous to him. He reported the fact to the officer in charge, who made an examination, and deciding that the area was safe, ordered Lennox back to his work.
>
> The convict, obeying, had not continued his work more than an hour when the roof fell in and completely buried him. He remained in this condition fully two hours. Missed at dinnertime, a search was instituted for the absent convict, and he was found under this heap of rubbish. He was taken from the mine, and on examination by the prison physician was pronounced dead. His remains were carried to the hospital, where he was washed and dressed preparatory for internment. His coffin was made and brought into the hospital. The chaplain had arrived to perform the last sad rites prior to burial. A couple of prisoners were ordered by the hospital steward to lift the corpse from the boards and carry it across the room and place it in the coffin. They obeyed, one at the head and the other at the feet, and were about half way across the room when the one who was at the head accidentally stumbled over a cuspidor, lost his balance and dropped the corpse.

The head of the dead man struck the floor, and to the utter surprise and astonishment of all present, a deep groan was heard. Soon the eyes opened, and other appearances of life were manifested. The physician was immediately sent for, and by the time he arrived, some thirty minutes, the dead man had called for a cup of water, and was in the act of drinking when the physician arrived. The coffin was at once removed, and later on was used to bury another convict. His burial robes were also taken from him, and the prison garb substituted. On an examination, he was found to have one of his legs broken in two places, and was otherwise bruised. He remained in the hospital some six months and again went to work.

Reynolds' book, printed in 1889, described the terrible conditions of prisoners. His book resulted in a statewide outcry against the barbaric conditions in every penal institution in Kansas. Prison life supposedly improved – but not enough for J. M. S. Thomas, the sixty-one-year-old doctor, to survive his sentence for raping young Effie Norlin.

With the Thomas sentencing interrupting the Lunney trial, Thomas' five-year prison term delivered to the Lunney jurors and the community a strong message about the seriousness of rape. It would be treated as a crime not condoned by at least one Norton County jury in 1894. Editor Conway wrote that rape was a crime in which "people have indulged no patience."

~

Nineteenth century women like Ellen Lunney revered their chastity, the sexual purity that made them distinct from the common woman of the street. Without their chastity, they fell into a different classification, a "fallen woman." A woman feared that no man who knew her history would accept her as a wife. In a small town like Lenora, Kansas, it was akin to wearing a red letter "A" on her forehead.

Growing up often proved to be difficult for young girls isolated on rural farms. They found their bodies changing but had only their mother or other girls to discuss what they felt. Boys, whether native-born or immigrants, found more opportunities, particularly if they fared well in school. Ellen had received more education than her brothers Tom and Will but had fewer opportunities. In the nineteenth century it was men who built the bridges and railroads. A man's morals and religious development might be neglected, but it was the woman's role to remind him of the goodness in the world when they were in the home and church.

In considering her professional future, Ellen had few options – teaching school being the common choice, except, of course, for finding a husband and preparing for life as a farm wife. She might obtain a "town" job, doing clerical work in a store or providing secretarial services to a lawyer or doctor. Ellen had selected teaching and had hoped to continue to live at home and teach in the fall, but so far no school had offered her a job.

Girls could date the opposite sex but needed to be wary of developing a reputation for being "fast" or "loose." Their teachers and family described the life of the farm wife as being devoid of sexual desire. Women were taught to concern themselves with domestic duties, love of home life and the responsibilities for raising children. Sexual intercourse was for procreation of the species, not for enjoyment. Purity manuals written at the time described menstrual cycles as "love's eternal wound," a monthly time to endure the fate of being born a female.

In this era of Victorian values, girls approaching marriageable age often had to work hard to court the attention of interested males. The chances remained few, mainly school, social events, church services, visits to other families and weekly trips to small towns to purchase supplies for the farm. Most of the courting occurred in public view. At all times girls needed to retain the patina of respectability and not become aligned too closely to any boy who they were unprepared to marry, which may account for Ellen's refusal to go out with Gene McEnroe. Gene lacked a job, and while he might be in line eventually to take over his father's farm, it was heavily mortgaged. And the farm house? It was half sod, years after frame lumber had become available by rail. As a prospect, Ellen could have found far better than Eugene McEnroe.

And could Ellen's rejection of Gene been the reason for her rape? Had Gene suffered enough because the snooty rich girl from

106

across the river had rejected him, and he needed to show his dominance with sex? Twentieth-century social scientists would argue that sexual coercion is motivated by power, not lust. The scientists say rape is not primarily a sexual crime but a crime of violence. For Dr. J. M. S. Thomas, sex with Effie Norlin may have resulted from passion although the law considered it rape because of her young age. Yet for Ellen Lunney, rape seemed more of an oppression, a means to control her, and perhaps a demonstration that a real man lived just across the river.

Girls wanted to be seen with desirable young men at public functions and might want to stake an early claim on the young man, although that limited the flexibility of going out with other men. Girls fared better if they made their pick of a potential mate as early as possible and did not change their minds.

Women in the nineteenth century tried to emulate the goals that society expected. Piety and purity of mind and body ranked high among those expectations. Women became the handmaidens of God, and their morals and actions often seemed to be have been taken from their church's version of the Bible. She needed to be submissive and domestic. Intellectual development must not interfere with her domestic role in the home.

Twenty-first-century historians describe Ellen and other nineteenth-century women as living in "the cult of domesticity," or "the cult of the lady." They characterize the ideal women depicted in magazines such as Godey's Lady's Book, religious books and popular culture as "true womanhood." When men went to their jobs, they helped create the view that men alone should provide financial support for the family. Taming the West, surviving in the world of business or building railroads and laying out new towns could become a rough job, and men did what they had to in order to succeed.

Men expected their women to be religious and pure of heart. Piety and purity stood as the core characteristics of a woman's virtue, the source of her strength. Without sexual purity, a woman proved to be no woman at all, and a fallen woman proved even worse. A fallen angel would be unworthy of a man's love. Wouldn't Ellen be considered at least a damaged angel by the local community?

Ellen had lost her greatest treasure, her virginity, and on her wedding night she no longer could give her husband her chastity. Gene McEnroe had assaulted her, stolen her purity and defiled her character. Lafe Thompson later would tell the jury of the example of the dying defiled virgin, saying that the woman ended her life in poverty. Other moralists would have added that the defiled woman had been punished by God, and they wouldn't be surprised should she lose her babies and become mad! A woman who allowed herself to be seduced by a man often atoned for the outrage by dying.

Ellen Lunney, truly, considered herself a ruined woman.

～

The development of a judicial system in western Kansas occurred about the same time as counties organized and cities incorporated. Yet at the same time the frontier continued its own style of justice that had been practiced for years, the rough vigilantism with citizens keeping their own brand of law and order when no other was available or when the system was not doing what the residents expected. The lynch law ruled the edge of the frontier, and for several years vigilante justice seemed to operate in parallel with the newly installed courtroom justice. In most cases, the crimes that attracted the vigilantes were horse stealing or murder, but in some cases the crime was rape. Those administering the vigilante law described it as the law imposed by Judge Lynch, an imaginary judicial authority giving them the power to hang, or lynch, the accused.

One study of 203 lynchings in Kansas between 1850 and 1900 found that most, ninety-three, were for horse stealing. The next reason was murder. Ranking third in a dead heat came rape and robbery. These lynchings began when Kansas still was unsettled. The prairie remained open and undeveloped, and cities, counties and courts often had not arrived in the settlements or rural areas where local governments eventually would be located. Most of the lynchings recorded happened during the 1860s when border war-

fare in the eastern part of the state accounted for much of the law-
lessness. But after the border fighting and Civil War ended, from
1870 to 1900 there was a steady decline in the number of lynchings
during each decade as a judicial system was placed into operation.
Lynchings in the southern United States may have been connected
with race, but on the western frontier it was a swift reaction to
horse thievery or, often, suspected thievery.

". . . The stealing of horses and other stock, though not so uni-
versally prevalent as formerly, is, I regret to say, still common in
nearly all parts of the state," said a disconsolate Kansas Governor
Thomas Carney in 1863.

Lynching also was the frontier's favorite punishment for rape.
Thirteen hangings from 1860 to 1900 listed in the study were for
rape.

Most murder cases involved men. One case of a woman convicted of murder in Osborne County occurred, and it was important because of the role science played in the conviction. Hiram
Cook died on his claim on Kill Creek township in 1876. His wife
Henrietta was suspected of poisoning her husband. She pleaded
not guilty in district court. The dead man's stomach was removed
and taken to the Agricultural College in Manhattan where an analysis found sufficient strychnine to produce death. A jury sat
through a nine-day trial and convicted Henrietta of murder in the
first degree. The death penalty was imposed, which a local newspaper said "under the operation of our statute is construed to mean
imprisonment for life."

～

Lafe Thompson and Clinton Angevine probably discussed at
least two different defenses to keep Ellen Lunney from being convicted of murder. One would have been justifiable homicide, a not
uncommon defense used on the frontier.

The American frontier had its own type of self defense. Under
English common law, a man had to be backed up against a wall and
faced with no choice but to defend himself because he had no
escape. Not so in the West. The threshold was different. All that

had to occur was for a man's honor, or a woman's honor, to be threatened. That was enough cause for a man or a lady to defend himself or herself.

Self defense might have appeared an acceptable defense for Ellen Lunney except for one significant problem. She waited a week before killing her attacker. Judge and jury liked to see the revenge, if it were to be bloody and involve a killing, to occur more quickly, particularly if the attacker lived just over the river in the next draw. The defense attorneys would counter that the McEnroes, particularly Patsey, spread stories that Ellen Lunney had been an unchaste woman and drove her to desperation, prompting her to shoot her attacker. That might account for the week's delay, they could argue. The attorneys also would change the terminology so they would be arguing "justifiable homicide" instead of calling it self-defense.

Thompson and Angevine would have discussed the temporary insanity defense. The prosecution was prepared to fight anything connecting the rape to the killing. But Angevine had adopted a clever strategy of bringing up the subject of insanity indirectly and would slip a few words about Ellen's responsibility into the defense's case before the prosecution understood what had happened.

~

Now it was the defense attorneys' turn. Clinton Angevine rose for his opening argument and spoke as if he were a man amazed at what had happened previously in the courtroom.

"The state directed all its force to the development of the shooting but never once voluntarily let out the reason for that unusual assemblage," said Angevine.

"I shall explain it."

With great skill and feeling, Angevine took the jurors back years in time, when John Lunney arrived in the United States as an Irish immigrant, when he married Anna Dunlap and "of the advent of the birth of the sweet little babe, first born to them, Ellen, the defendant at the bar, and all the hopes built upon her future."

110

The attorney told how the young Lunney couple, after the birth of Ellen on June 17, 1875, based "all the hopes of the future on the little girl, her moral nature and her mind cultured to the best in womanhood" as she grew to a young woman, and how she was a graduate of the Norton County high school system. Angevine focused on Ellen's education and the fact that she had been granted a teaching certificate. He told the jurors that Ellen "had spent a term teaching school, her future outlined with good hope's roseate hues – only to have it all blasted away in a night."

"The appalling gloom that fell upon the family is beyond the portraiture of words," he said.

The jury watched a talented lawyer trained in the eloquence of nineteenth century oratory. A legal history of Smith County, Kansas, describes Angevine as one of the best young lawyers in the county, and it was easy to see why he moved to the more populous Kansas City to practice his skills, leaving the small courthouses of western Kansas to others with lesser talents.

Angevine told the jury:

> On Tuesday night, July 24, Patsey and Dan McEnroe were over to the Lunneys and remained with the two Lunney boys, Tom and Will, until about eleven o'clock, waiting for the return of John Lunney, his wife and the smaller children who had gone fifteen miles away on a visit.
>
> At this hour Ellen retired to her room upstairs and went to bed, remarking to the four boys that the parents would not come home that night or they would have appeared earlier.
>
> The McEnroe boys left for their home. Afterwards, in a few hours, Eugene McEnroe came to the Lunney house, opened the screen door by breaking the screen opposite the latch, entering the house, going upstairs to the bedroom of the defendant, finding her there in bed asleep, the moonlight pouring in through the window, making the room almost as light as day.
>
> And then getting into bed and raping the defendant. The ceiling was so low and in her struggle to escape him she skinned her knees.
>
> When she tried to scream, he clamped his hand over her mouth. After accomplishing his purpose, he went downstairs, ran around by the east window toward the corn cribs, in plain view of the defendant, running a distance of six or eight rods (thirty-three to forty-four yards) and disappeared.

She immediately wrapped a quilt about her and went down to the granary and woke the boys. They immediately called the dogs and fired the guns.

The next day she and her father went to Squire Thuma and had Eugene arrested. At the preliminary hearing he was bound over until July 31 on $1,000 bond, which she understood he could not give. But the next day she saw him, across the river in the adjoining field, cutting corn. And later she found that, after leaving the squire's place, his bond was reduced.

Following on the heels of this incident came the stories of unchastity – reports that she was a bad woman, that all the crimes of lewdness and want of decency were laid upon her. This so worked upon her, so aggravated her that she thought it was a scheme to free Eugene McEnroe, the author of her ruin.

These vicious scandals harassed her to desperation, and their accumulation drove her to melancholy. She went to the preliminary hearing not expecting to find him, but finding him there, and on first meeting him face to face to see that triumphant leer on his face, the sneer, the laugh of mockery – I say if Ellen Lunney was not Ellen Lunney when she made those shots, she could not have committed murder – that it was God who directed her arm and also to end the dastardly career of the author of her ruin.

Angevine's words to the jury drew no reaction or objection from the prosecution. Jones and Wilder would learn later why the words were so important. It implied temporary madness without saying it, without giving the prosecution an opportunity to directly refute that Ellen Lunney had been so distraught that she became mentally unbalanced. Perhaps the awkward construction of Angevine's statement caused the prosecution to miss the importance of his words. As John William Conway of the *Norton Champion* noted:

> Mr. Angevine spoke at some length in presenting the line of defense, but the only intimation that irresistible impulses, emotional insanity or temporary loss of reason and will power were to be resorted to in the defense, was the hypothetical statement, "if Ellen Lunney was not Ellen Lunney ..."

It seems the full impact of this phrase of the defense was not then realized by the state because Colonel Jones later on in objecting to the introduction of the rape episode in the tragic tale argued its incompetency, irrelevancy and immateriality unless in cases where insanity was pleaded; whereupon Mr. Angevine called his attention to this foregoing remark, and made it plainer by the reassertion that she did not know what she was doing, or in the words of witness Abraham Hendricks, "did not realize what she had done."

~

When the trial reconvened on Thursday morning, Lafe Thompson moved, before the jurors were seated in the courtroom, to dismiss John McKeniff and Tom Lunney as defendants. Thompson said the state had not shown that they were in any way connected with the homicide and that the evidence was not sufficient to hold them in custody. Thompson said he desired the two as witnesses but could not call them until they were discharged as defendants.

Wilder opposed the motion and laid the weight of the guilt for the homicide on Tom Lunney and John McKeniff. Wilder said John McKeniff and Tom Lunney, were "more guilty than the girl." The two young men had become the only remaining links that the prosecution had to demonstrate how a conspiracy of the Lunney family and John McKeniff led to the death of Gene McEnroe.

The prosecution did not want to lose the two young men as defendants. In 1894 women of the plains were not expected to protect themselves. That was the job of their husbands and brothers. The prosecution wanted to lay as much blame at the feet of McKeniff and young Tom Lunney as possible. Women were passed, often with little voice in the matter, from the protection of their fathers to the protection of their husbands. If their husbands died, they either found new husbands to protect them or their brothers, or their church, had the responsibility. If the defense proved skillful, Angevine and Thompson might persuade the jurors that the girl was a sympathetic person and conceivably could free her or convict her of a lesser charge, but at least the prosecutors believed they still would have Tom Lunney and the McKeniff boy facing a conviction.

Prosecutor C. D. Jones joined the debate and outlined the circumstances of McKeniff's and Tom Lunney's guilt. He argued the boys waited outside the school so they could flee on horseback or by wagon with Ellen.

Angevine then argued that if he were the jury, he could not have found from the evidence beyond a reasonable doubt that Tom Lunney and John McKeniff were guilty of murder.

The *Norton Champion* described what happened next.

> [Judge Geiger] weighed the testimony of both sides with a marvelous display of judicial reasoning. In the progress of the discussion the imaginary balance tipped and swayed, rose and sunk as doubt followed certainty and certainty followed doubt until few, if any, in the courtroom could anticipate the final judgment of the court. The judgment was in harmony with the opinions of the audience among whom the whispering rose like a murmuring tide.

The judgment, said Geiger, was to dismiss the charges against John McKeniff and Tom Lunney.

Dismissal of the charges would have brought renewed optimism to the defense counsels' table. Ellen saw her first glimpse of hope, the first indication that everything the prosecution had been saying may not be believed by everyone in the courtroom. Her spirits would have risen, her shoulders straightened and for the first time since the trial began she could have sat upright at the defense table. With John McKeniff and Tom Lunney freed from the charges of being an accessory to the crime, the message was clear to the jury: the case was not as strong as the prosecution claimed. Dismissal of the charge hampered the prosecution's argument that a family's conspiracy lurked behind the crime, and that young Tom and McKeniff stood as the main perpetrators of it. The defense now had the option of using the two young men as witnesses in the trial without fears that they could incriminate themselves. They were free to tell their stories to the jury.

But strangely, even after the dismissal, the prosecution neglected to delete the two young defendants from the information charging the crime. Perhaps the prosecution was too preoccupied, too busy to bother to amend the charges before sending the court's material to the jury. It would remain for Geiger to explain the inclusion in his jury instructions.

Ten

The defense called its first witness, Benjamin J. Marsh, a thirty-two-year-old photographer who was asked to identify some photographs he had taken of the Lunney house and surroundings. The prosecutors objected, saying the Lunney premises were not in any way connected to the case. The defense argued that the rape occurred in the Lunney house, and the rape itself was a justification of the conduct of Ellen Lunney. The photographs would give the jury a good view of where the events occurred, said the defense.

Judge Geiger agreed with the defense and allowed the photographs to be introduced. Marsh testified that the granary in exhibit A "stood six or eight rods southeast of the residence." The defense handed the photos to the jury after the prosecution's objection was overruled.

Then, after dinner (on the plains they called the noonday meal dinner; they called the evening meal "supper") the defense called Ellen Lunney to the witness stand. She would be the key witness. Much depended upon her being reliable and believable and her story being accepted by the twelve male jurors.

~

Ellen Lunney literally had grown up in a tiny area of western Kansas, her neighborhood as she knew it. There is no indication she or her family traveled far from where she opened her eyes in 1875. If she knew what was happening in the rest of America or the world, it would only be through what she had learned in school or read in books, magazines or newspapers.

Ellen sat in the witness chair, probably feeling small and terribly lonely, surrounded by the dark wood and white walls of the courtroom with an audience of anxious eyes staring at her in rapt attention. The weight of the world looked to be on her shoulders as she took center stage, her life in the balance, and she and everybody in the packed courtroom knew it.

Clinton Angevine stepped forward and began by asking easy questions to settle her nerves and help her gain some confidence before settling in to answering the hardest questions of her life. "My name is Ellen Lunney. I am nineteen years old. I was born in Kansas, Norton County, and I resided all my life in Almelo township, except for two years when I lived on a farm one and a half miles south of my present home," the defendant told the packed courtroom in response to questions by her Angevine.

Ellen was the trial's star witness, and Angevine and Thompson had decided they wanted her on the witness stand as soon as they opened their defense.

Ellen described her study toward a teaching certificate, which she received on July twenty, 1893. She had taught three terms and intended to teach this winter.

Angevine asked her about her church and her family.

"I am a member of the Catholic church," she said. Angevine moved quickly to explore her social life. "I never went with any men except my brothers, cousins and lady friends." Once, she said, she went with her cousin John McKeniff about seven miles, but it was midday on a public highway. She never went with him "or any other fellow" unless her family accompanied her.

"I always consulted my parents when I went to any entertainment, and I never went without their consent," Ellen said.

The little cities on the High Plains provided culture through literary societies, social clubs, church activities and visiting theater groups. The monotony of small towns and rural areas alike may have been broken a little by readings of a popular or classic book by one of the more intellectual elite of the community or by a political debate or spelling bee. Groups often organized themselves into thespian societies to present a play, and in temperance-conscious Kansas it could easily have been "Ten Nights in a Bar Room."

Lenora frequently discussed the need for a theater or auditorium where plays or visiting performances could be viewed.

Some of the farm wives joined women's town clubs, but there is no indication Anna Lunney belonged to any of the groups unless they were church-related. Ellen would have been arriving at the adult age where she could be joining such organized activities. The clubs provided outlets for women with leisure time, and that prohibited many of the busier farm wives from joining. Some managed to find time to attend book study groups, lectures on etiquette and proper table manners or visiting cultural performances in town.

In winter the lyceum, or literary society, attracted both women and men to town or rural schoolhouses. Programs included recitations by students or adults, songs and dialogues. Young musicians showed off their ability to play their instruments or sing popular or traditional songs. Political debates found large numbers of adult attendees, especially if a political issue or candidates for public office was on the agenda. Sometimes local representatives would stand in for candidates for statewide or national office and argue their man's position on the main issues of the day. In 1894, this included the populist platform, women's suffrage, prohibition, the shortage of money, the wisdom of an income tax on the wealthy, the state of the economy and the cause of the great Panic of '93. Debaters made unsupported arguments often thought up on the spot, speaking as loudly and vehemently as possible, hoping the strength of their voice would pass for a lack of factual information on an issue.

Above all, farmers and townspeople gathered to pass along the latest gossip and news. The town newspapers printed news items about the community and included as many names as they could. It was usual for a local editor to attend gatherings in search of news items that would appear in the weekly publication.

~

On July 24, 1894, Ellen said she was at home when her family decided to visit relatives, the McKenna family. "I wanted my sister, Mary, to stay with me, but she begged and cried to go with my mother. They left about eight or nine o'clock in the morning and went more than ten miles west to visit my aunt and uncle. They are old acquaintances and it was usual to visit back and forth. Mother and father did not know if they would be back that night."

Angevine asked questions about the Lunney house.

She described her house as having two upstairs bedrooms. Normally, she slept in the west bedroom with her sister Mary. Her two brothers Tom and Will slept in the east bedroom, but in warm weather the boys slept in the granary. That night she slept alone in the east bedroom.

It was common on the High Plains for men to look for a cooler spot to spend the hot summer nights. Some families built sleeping porches. Wagons or outbuildings also were favorite places to try to avoid the summer heat.

"John McKeniff?" He lived with his brother Hugh a mile south in a sod house, which she could not see from the Lunney house because it is located "in a draw." McKeniff had not been at the Lunney house during the previous two weeks and she had not seen him in that time. As to how he looked, McKeniff "wore a mustache but no whiskers."

Ellen described the location of the Lunney's house as being on the upland from the Solomon River, which runs generally west to east. The river bank begins to break just below the corn crib, and "it drops considerably. There is quite a bank there. The side hill is about as high as this room, and it slopes to the south" before it flattens and is level to the river.

"James McEnroe?" Ellen said she was "well acquainted" with the entire McEnroe family and named all the children and gave their ages. Besides the river, a two-strand, barbed wire fence separates the McEnroes' house from the Lunney home. The farms join on the south and west. The McEnroes' home is located about a quarter mile away and is even closer to the river than the Lunney home.

She never "kept company" with Eugene McEnroe although "four years ago he asked for my company and two years later did the same. Eugene asked me to go with him, but I wouldn't. He kept coming to the house."

Angevine brought the questioning back to the Lunney home.

"Our main door faces south," she said, "and the stairway is back of the door. It opens back against the stairway. In addition to the ordinary door, there's a screen door."

Angevine questioned Ellen about the events of July 24, and she testified:

"Dan McEnroe was at our house. He came in the afternoon. He ate supper with us, my two brothers, too. After supper Patsy McEnroe came, and before sundown Mr. Coleman came in the evening. I had never seen him before that I know of. My brothers and the two McEnroe boys chored and milked. About ten o'clock they went to the well, the pump. All the four boys were there. Tom asked me then if our parents would come home that night. I told him, no, because if they were coming they would be here by now."

Ellen said she "entered the house, took a light upstairs, blew it out and went to bed. I fastened the wire door but left the windows open as it was hot. With the wire door latched, I went to sleep. I am a sound sleeper. I went to sleep soon after going to bed."

The state objected to the testimony as a sound sleeper, and Ellen told of efforts of others to awaken her at different times, and "how hard it is." Her sister Mary, "a great kicker, usually sleeps with me."

Angevine asked: "After you went to sleep, when did you next awaken?" The state objected on the grounds of "irrelevancy and incompetency" and the jury was sent out of the room.

At that point one of the key arguments in the trial erupted. It concerned whether the rape of Ellen Lunney could be an excuse, or the reason, for the shooting and murder of Gene McEnroe, and whether her defense could be considered a justifiable homicide.

Wilder argued against admission of her testimony relating to the rape. He said there was "ample time for cooling between the rape and the homicide." He cited several cases where the longest time that elapsed between the provocation and the killing was six hours. He argued that the rape was not a palliation, a justification or an excuse for the homicide.

Colonel Jones added that the only way the evidence could be

introduced was to prove that the person lost her reason from the rape and was, at the time of the murder, insane, out of her mind or acting through an uncontrollable impulse. In this case, a week had passed since the alleged rape.

Angevine disagreed, saying the defense could offer the evidence of the rape as leading to the "excusable homicide." He cited a statute that homicide is justifiable under sufficient provocation. He cited one case where a general killed a man several days after he caught the man intimate with his wife. Angevine told of another case in which a father was killed trying to avenge his daughter's seduction, but several days later the brother and son killed the seducer and were acquitted. In both cases, the "cooling time" was much longer than six hours.

The time could be extended "almost indefinitely," said Angevine. He cited a Georgia case where a justifiable homicide occurred six years after an offense.

Then Jones rose again and told the court that "the doctrine of cooling time" actually was established in England's courts at the time of Charles the Second, and he argued that no crime could be avenged more than six hours after it occurred.

On and on the argument went. The debate between the four lawyers lasted nearly two hours, "and the great audience gave a sigh of relief when the court took the matter under consideration," the *Norton Champion* reported.

Judge Geiger took a break, returned and ruled on the key question by saying that "excusable homicide" means something to be determined by the jury.

"Every case is peculiar to itself and should be examined for its own developments," Geiger said. He overruled the state's objection, and noted the state's exception. The jury would decide if the rape was material or if it even occurred.

The judge told the bailiff to recall the jury.

Eleven

After Geiger's ruling, the judge recalled the jury and Ellen Lunney again took her seat in the witness chair. For her, this would be a long and important session. She needed to establish that she was honest and forthright. And she needed the jury to believe her and her story of the rape. Above all, she had to persuade the jury that she should not be convicted of murder for her reaction to the rape.

"When did you next awaken?" Clint Angevine asked Ellen, to which she replied,

> I awoke about twelve o'clock. A sharp pain awakened me. Eugene McEnroe lay on top of me. He put his hand to my mouth when I tried to scream. I struggled and in turning scratched my knees on the low ceiling. In tussling I found myself lying crosswise on the bed. His face was close to mine. His right hand was over my mouth. He lay upon me, between my limbs. The penetration into my body is what woke me up.
>
> How did I know it was Eugene McEnroe?
>
> I am well acquainted with Eugene McEnroe. I know it was Eugene McEnroe. There was moonlight through the east window. My bed was about three feet from the window, and the light of the moon shown upon the head of the bed. When he got off the bed he passed through the moonlight down stairs.
>
> I knew it was Eugene McEnroe when I woke up. It was a calm night. When he went downstairs I got up from the bed and saw him go toward the corn crib. I saw him till he went out of sight behind the corn crib that stood southeast of the house a few rods. He wore a light colored shirt.
>
> When he got out of view I went down stairs and went to call the boys in the granary. Tom awoke after being called twice. I told him Eugene McEnroe had been in the house, told him he went down behind the corn crib. Tom got his gun and shot it off and called the dogs. I could easily see objects about the yard or the corn crib as the night was bright.

Angevine asked when this occurred.

"A little after or before midnight," she said. "Tom told Willie that Eugene McEnroe had been in the house. He asked if Eugene took any money, or if there was any money in the house.

"I told him he got something worse than money, and he guessed my meaning," she said.

What was she wearing to bed?

"That night I wore drawers, a chemise and gown." A pair of torn drawers were identified as the ones worn that night and introduced into evidence. "The drawers are in the same condition as they were then. I cannot say whether the stains were caused that night. I was just getting over my monthlies. The drawers were washed since then by my mother."

Blood stains on the drawers from her monthlies? The woman would not have been pregnant if she sustained her monthly period.

"I did not sleep until very late the next morning. I lay awake thinking. I cried till morning and was much troubled in the mind about it.

"During the struggle in the bed plastering was knocked down," she said. "My knees were skinned and sore for a couple of weeks after."

"My parents came home the next day. It was my custom to meet them on arriving, but I did not go out to meet them at this time. Willie and Tom met them. When they entered Willie and Thomas were crying. Father and mother inquired as to the trouble. I told them. I was crying. We all were crying. I told them what had happened as soon as I could do so for my crying."

Angevine asked what happened next.

"I went with my father to Squire Thuma's. He lives northeast of our place," Ellen said. "To have Eugene McEnroe arrested."

Thuma, the justice of the peace, was not at home so they went instead to Lenora.

"We went to Squire Hendricks and had Eugene arrested on the charge of rape that day," Ellen said. "The trial was postponed to July 31. Eugene was bound over in the sum of $1,000, which, it was understood, was not given."

Justices of the peace often were called "squire," a term of courtesy and respect.

~

The court recessed for the night. The next day, Friday, Ellen resumed her testimony. Angevine continued questioning her.

My brother Tom went over to Thuma's the following day and found that the bonds had been reduced. I saw Eugene the next day in the cornfield in front of our house. He was cutting corn. It was in plain view of the house. There was talk between me and mother in regard to his being out there. My brother and McKeniff were at Thuma's the next morning. They said the bond was reduced and Gene had given bond and was at liberty. I thought that it was a scheme for him to get clear.

After coming from Squire Thuma's, I asked Tom to teach me to shoot. I never shot a pistol before getting the revolver. My father had a revolver but I never shot it. I don't know whether it was double or single action. In fact I don't know the difference between them. Father's revolver is something like the one shown in court.

On Thursday, after coming from Squire Thuma's, Tom went to Lenora. I told him to buy me a revolver. My brother had told me my father's revolver was hard to pull off, and that I could not shoot with it. Thursday evening he bought me a revolver. It looks like the revolver introduced here. I saw it in the bureau drawer and used it the next day. That evening my brother and I went down to the timber to learn to shoot. He loaded it for me and I shot at a stump of a tree. I shot three or four times but did not hit it. It was about sundown or a little after. We went back to the house and did not fire the revolver again. We did the shooting about one hundred rods from the house.

Were other guns in the house?

My people keep two or three guns in the house, double-barreled shotguns. Had them ever since I can remember. The boys used them to hunt quite often.

The McEnroes stopped coming to the house.

The McEnroes had girls about my age. I knew them ever since I knew the family. These girls frequently visited our house. The visiting occurred up to the time of the rape. They never came after that.

I was distressed after the rape, worked up, worried. I thought that I was ruined and degraded. Some neighbors came in to see us. Mr. and Mrs. Thuma. Sadie Gilleece. I thought they intentionally avoided me.

Mr. and Mrs. McKenna. I told them what happened.

On Friday evening, my mother told me there were reports about my character. She said that the reports were in circulation after the rape. She said that the reports started from the McEnroes. These reports had a great effect on my feelings. I thought they were trying to get out these reports and lie about me to clear this fellow Eugene McEnroe.

On the next Monday my mother told me of other reports, that I was a bad woman, that my cousin John McKeniff was running with me for six months, that I had got into trouble by being intimate with John McKeniff. At the time of the rape I had my monthlies. I had just got over being unwell. My mother told me that Patsey McEnroe started the story and who he told it to, and of the different sources as it came to her. The language of her report was too bad to use here.

"On the morning of July 31, at eight o'clock, I left in a lumber wagon with father and mother for Thuma's. Prior to July 31, in the latter part of that week, John McKeniff remained at our house. He was sick," she said, remembering instructions from her lawyers about the family's carriage being a lumber wagon instead of a more fashionable spring wagon.

The fact that John McKeniff had stayed at the house recently was not something the defense lawyers wanted to be brought out by a prosecution witness. It would be better to be mentioned in Ellen Lunney's testimony because of talk about her relationship with him.

"There was no relationship between me and McKeniff other than what would exist between brother and sister," Ellen said in reply to a question by Angevine.

She was asked about the pistol purchased by McKeniff and her brother.

"I put the revolver in my pocket," she said. "I bought it to protect myself. Every time I left the house I took the revolver with me."

"We did not stay long at Thuma's," she added. "The McEnroes were there," she said to explain the reason for the short stay. "From there we went to the school house."

"John McKeniff was at the house on that morning. We left him, Tom and Willie at the house. I next saw them at Thumas."

Ellen was asked when she next saw McKeniff.

THE HIGH PLAINS SAGA OF A WOMAN'S REVENGE

"I saw him at Thumas. I did not talk with him. I next saw him at the school house after the shooting. I did not see him before at the school house nor did I speak to him until after the shooting. McKeniff was not in our wagon."

What happened next at the Thuma School?

> We got out and went into the school house. We didn't stop to talk to anyone as we went to the school. Our team stopped at the northeast corner of the school house. The door is on the south. None but father, mother and myself rode in the wagon.
>
> I was worried to have to tell my story in the school house before all those people. I was greatly agitated. I had no thought then or prior to that of killing Eugene McEnroe, nor at any time before.
>
> We stood looking for a seat and I saw Eugene McEnroe grin and leer at me. I don't know that I can describe my feelings or the sensation that possessed me. Seeing him there increased my agitation.
>
> I know I walked up to him. I don't know what else I did do. I don't remember whether I shot or not. I did not know who was around me, except that I was in a crowd. I have no recollection of how I got out of the school house or anything about it until I sat in the buggy.
>
> I don't remember anyone taking a revolver from me. In the buggy I noticed the skin was knocked off my thumb. I don't know how it occurred. I did not see Regester or Miller, nor did I know that they took the revolver. I have no remembrance of it. I know there was a crowd about me, but I could not recognize anyone. I did not hear anyone speak.
>
> At the wagon I saw John McKeniff. Not before. I don't know how I got to the buggy or in it. From that time to the next Saturday I was with Squire Darnell. Since then I have been at Mr. Betterton's or in jail.

She was asked if there were any stains on the bed clothes. Ellen replied that there were blood stains from her sister, who had a nosebleed the night before "Gene had been there."

Ellen's testimony that she had "no thought then or prior to that of killing Eugene McEnroe" went to the heart of the premeditation that everyone must have assumed was in her mind. Not only did her testimony – if it held up under cross examination – seem harmful to the prosecution's case, but her seemingly lack of a memory about the events laid the groundwork for her attorneys to talk about temporary insanity or "unaccountability."

∽

Next it was Ledru Wilder's turn to cross-examine Ellen Lunney. He asked first about her education and the courses she had studied. She named several, including history, geography, penmanship and arithmetic. She admitted she studied mathematics "no higher" than arithmetic, studied none of the languages except English and received her diploma from the "county authorities."

Ellen said she held a "third-grade certificate." This was a type of certificate developed by the state of Kansas' educational system, and it was the lowest of three types of certificates that teachers could receive. Wilder went out of his way to point out that it was "only a third-grade certificate." A third-grade certificate allowed the individual to teach for one year. As a comparison, a second-grade certificate was good for two years and required the applicant to pass a test. The first-grade certificate, allowing teachers to ply their trade for three years, required the applicant to pass a test to show proficiency in orthography, reading, writing, English grammar, composition, geography and arithmetic. Young teachers were encouraged to move from a third-grade certificate to a first as rapidly as possible.

"Moving up" would require Ellen to attend one of Kansas' six normal schools, the closest of which were in Salina or Great Bend, more than a hundred miles away, or to attend the University of Kansas at Lawrence, more than two hundred miles distant.

Higher education in Kansas remained in its infancy in the 1890s. By 1893 the University of Kansas at Lawrence enrolled 691 students. The agricultural college at Manhattan enrolled one hundred less, and the average attendance that year at the normal schools was about 500. One of the normal schools, a popular one in Emporia, attracted 1,231 students. During the year, 9,180 local schools enrolled a total of 398,000 students in all educational endeavors. Lenora schools in 1893 offered nine years of common school work and two years of high school.

Ellen had taught three terms of school, the first when she was 17. All the schools were rural and in the southwest or northwest part of Norton County. The school year lasted four to five months in all the rural, one- or two-room schools where she taught.

The Kansas Legislature had decreed that school districts should maintain a system of common schools that would be open for "not less than four months" between the first of October and the first day of June. If the school district's board should neglect or refuse to provide funds for these schools, it became the duty of the county superintendent, in conjunction with the county commissioners, to place a levy on the tax roll of that district to provide for the schools.

Norton County had a rudimentary school system organized soon after the county was settled in 1872. The early school buildings were dugouts, sod houses or log cabins, but by 1893 most of the schools were in frame buildings. Norton, Almena, Lenora and Edmond maintained grade schools, and sentiment grew for establishing a county high school. It would be built soon in Norton, with a countywide tax levy that would cause farmers outside the county seat to complain that they were paying to educate someone else's children. Even if a county high school were approved in the November general election, the distance from New Almelo, Lenora or Densmore to Norton was far enough to make it difficult for students to attend without boarding with someone in the county seat.

~

Wilder wanted to know if Ellen Lunney traveled to the schools each day from home. His questions at this point were exploratory, as if he hoped to find some fertile ground for the prosecution's case.

"I boarded some of the time," she said. "I was never away from home more than a month."

"I taught three terms of school. All the schools are in the southwest or northwest of the county, about six or seven miles from home," Ellen said. When questioned that the schools may have been even farther from her home, Ellen confessed that "I'm not a good judge of distance. I taught in the Matt Linden district first, the next in the Lease district, five miles west of home, west or southwest, I don't know which."

Wilder had gained an acknowledgement from Ellen that she was not a good judge of distance, an important concession when the prosecution contended that she had difficulty identifying her attacker. He turned his attention to the layout of the Lunney farm.

"The Solomon River runs on the south side of our house," she replied to the prosecutor's question.

How far from the house is the river?

"About 75 rods," she said, indicating it stood ten times as far as its true distance. To test her knowledge – and to make a point of her unreliability in determining distances – Wilder asked Ellen to tell the jury how far was the state bank building, which was visible across the street from the courtroom. How far was another building?

How far was the corn crib from the Lunney house?

"Fifty-three yards," she said. "The granary is forty-nine yards. I remember from being told."

How tall are the trees along the river?

"The trees along the river are large and small," Ellen said. "The trees in diameter? That's unknown to me."

"What kind are they?"

"Box elder, ash, elm, willow. Oh yes, and cottonwoods," she added.

Wilder asked about the size of the house. He was confusing Ellen, putting her on the defensive and making progress in weakening her credibility as a witness.

"Our house is two stories with a kitchen to the north. The door of the kitchen is in the west. No other doors are on the west side. The other door is to the south. There are no other outside doors."

Wilder then began a series of questions about the location of Ellen's room and whether the moonlight on the night of July 24 would have allowed her to see the identity of the person who raped her. The answers did little to show Wilder's contention that the moonlight on the night in question was insufficient to allow Ellen to tell if Eugene McEnroe was the person in her room and the same person she saw in the farmyard.

Angevine, on redirect examination, showed a photo of the farmyard in an effort to blunt any idea that the victim could not have seen or identified her rapist.

"I can see the corn crib but not behind it," Ellen said. "I could see him go around the crib. I think it is five or six yards from the crib to the edge of the bank that leads to the river, and the bank is about sixty or seventy-five yards from the house."

Angevine asked again about the events of the evening. Ellen said she assisted in milking the Lunney's cows and in the straining of the milk that followed.

"They brought in the milk and I put it away," she said. "I don't remember whether I strained each batch separately."

The questions then turned to how much she struggled during the attack.

"I struggled all I could when he was there. I felt sore all over afterwards. My arms and wrists were sore, and my legs were sore.

"As soon as he went downstairs I went to the east window. I was afraid to go downstairs. I did not start down because I was afraid until I saw him pass the crib," she said.

How much did Ellen weigh?

"The last time I was weighed I weighed 124 pounds."

Angevine asked when John McKeniff arrived at the house the next day.

"McKeniff came over to our house with Willie because Will had gone to tell him what had occurred. McKeniff came before my parents arrived.

"I don't remember who came in first," she said. "I was crying. I cried all the week about my ruin. I prayed a great deal to God to help me in what course to pursue. I came near to committing suicide that week."

That ended Ellen Lunney's testimony. Wilder had managed to confuse Ellen about distance, but he did not seem to make many other points helpful to the prosecution. Ellen had held up well, but she could be recalled to clear up testimony from other witnesses. Her time in the witness chair had not ended although the defense began calling other witnesses.

～

Seywood Larrick, the Lenora banker who had been a witness for the state, was recalled. He said he told John McKeniff about July 28 that there were reports out about him and Ellen, "reports that were derogatory to their character." The prosecution objected. Judge Geiger agreed. The testimony was stricken as hearsay.

~

Effie Norlin, also a state's witness, was recalled. Although she lived two miles east of Lenora, she had known Ellen Lunney for several years, attended school with her and roomed with her while Ellen attended normal school, "a month each time or three months in all" in 1890, 1891 and 1892. Effie said Ellen sleeps "very sound." When someone went out of the room or came in "some would awaken but Ellen would not know until the next morning when we came in. We girls talked frequently about it."

Effie also said she was aware of Ellen Lunney's reputation "as to being a moral, virtuous and upright girl," she said. "She has always borne a good reputation, and she never exhibited an immodest act in all my school acquaintance with her."

At that point the defense recalled Ellen Lunney to the witness stand to testify about the revolver and to counter some of Effie Norlin's earlier testimony about the shooting. As a prosecution witness, Effie said that Ellen had told her that if she had to do it over, "she would do it again."

As for talking to Effie Norlin at the Betterton's house, Ellen denied some of a conversation she supposedly had with Effie.

"I stayed at Betterton's and saw Effie Norlin up there. I did not tell Effie Norlin that I was not certain that I shot the right person, that it was not very light and that I could not see very well," Ellen said.

~

The defense called several witnesses to describe the weather on the night of the rape, trying to show that it was a bright, light night, or to testify about Ellen's character and reputation.

Barney Hickert, a neighbor who lived a half mile northeast of the Lunneys, testified that he remembered hearing shooting during the week of the attack.

"It was hot and I had a kind of hammock that I slept in," said

130

Hickert. "It was either the 24th or 25th. It was in the direction of the Lunney house that I heard two shots."

∽

The defense called S. P. Allway, who lived five miles east of the Lunneys.

"My house is probably ten rods from the Solomon River," Allway said. "I remember the night of the twenty-fourth of July last. The moon rose about ten or eleven o'clock. It rose northeast. It was as nice and bright a night as I ever saw. I could see objects very plain. I could tell objects fifty or one hundred rods. I could distinguish a person that I was acquainted with at least fifty yards. I had no lamp lit. The moon made a light in the house. It was very light and bright."

∽

The defense then called a series of witnesses to describe the character of Ellen Lunney.

Rissa Smith, who had roomed with Ellen in Norton and had known her for six years, said Ellen was a "very sound sleeper, as much as anyone I have ever known."

"I am acquainted with the character of Ellen," Rissa said. "I have never known anything against her. She attended my school for two winters. Her demeanor was always like a lady. I never knew of her acting in an indiscreet manner."

She was asked about the night of July 24.

"I was suffering with my teeth on the 24th," she said to explain how she recalled the night on that date. "I would say it was a cloudless, bright, moonlit night."

∽

A Mrs. Graham, with whom Ellen lived in Lenora while going to school "since the spring of ninety-two," was called. "Her reputation is good. She was at my house between eight and nine months. I never saw any indiscretion on her part during that time. Ellen never kept company with anyone. She gave strict attention to her studies. Her general conduct was good." Ellen was at the Graham house from September 1893 to May 1894.

~

Minnie Ferguson, who knew Ellen Lunney for six years, roomed with her at Graham's for about two weeks. She said Ellen was a "very sound sleeper" and had a good character.

~

O. M. Becker, who taught school at Lenora, knew her for four years.

"She is in every respect a perfect lady and her reputation is excellent. She is modest, timid rather than reserved. She was very studious and talked to me about her desire to become a good teacher."

~

E. F. Coleman, the horse trader who was at the Lunney farm for an hour or an hour and a half on the evening of July 24, said he was told Mr. and Mrs. Lunney were not at home. The "stranger," who Ellen had never seen before, reported seeing the Lunney boys and Dan and Patsey McEnroe. He arrived at the Lunneys about "half past seven" and "it was eight or nine when I left." He saw John McKeniff that evening en route to the Lunneys and asked for directions.

"I don't know where he lived," Coleman said. "He was going away from the Lunneys."

Coleman was asked about his own appearance and if he wore a mustache at the time. Coleman said he did, which would mark him as a suspect. Ellen's attacker also wore a mustache.

As to his own whereabouts, Coleman said he "stayed at my own house that night." He was alone at home.

On cross examination, Coleman said he understood Mr. and Mrs. Lunney were coming home that night. Why was he there?

"I was there with a stallion," and there was some talk about horses. "I went there to breed mares. That was all my business." He said he met John McKeniff and "a few words passed. We talked for five or ten minutes. I simply asked the way to the Lunneys. I was going north and he was going south."

A meeting between Coleman and McKeniff, both of whom would later become suspects in the rape of Ellen Lunney.

∽

Mrs. Catherine Peak was recalled. She said she had known the Lunney family for more than twenty years and was present when Ellen was born.

"I have been in company with Ellen a great many times," Mrs. Peak said. "I never saw an indiscreet act on her part. She is a very modest, timid girl and very ladylike in her demeanor. Rather exceptionally so."

∽

Robert Regester, a neighbor and a state witness, was recalled. He said he had known John McKeniff for two years.

"I live a fourth of a mile from his brother's place, where he stays."

Regester said he took the revolver from Ellen after the shooting and said he saw John Lunney inside the door. He had testified earlier that he heard John Lunney say, "She's done her work. She's done her work."

But no one else testified to have heard John Lunney utter those words or saw Ellen's father inside the school, and the words may have alerted the defense counsel that it may be unwise to have the father called as a witness.

Angevine jumped to his feet to cross examine. He won a major point when Regester expressed uncertainty that it was John Lunney inside the school. It would have been John McKeniff, and, yes, he must have been mistaken when he said it was John Lunney, Regester said.

Angevine left the subject and witness as soon as he could. He hoped the jury would not link John Lunney with the words, "She's done her work. She's done her work." Of course, one never knows what will be remembered by jurors, who must try to sort through a confusing group of faces and names and recall who said what.

The prosecution also left the words to be digested by the jury rather than to try to find out why she had done "her work" and whether anyone had discussed "her work" before the day of the killing in the Thuma School House. Sometimes, the contents of a can opened should be left to the imagination rather than examined.

At that point an almanac was introduced into evidence by the defense. The almanac was the prairie's traditional bible on weather and miscellaneous data such as the time of sunrise, sunset and the rising of the moon over the western hemisphere. The almanac said the moon rose at ten thirty-five that night, and the last quarter of the moon was the next day, July 25.

~

Wilhelmine Mindrup was next to be called. A neighbor, she lived a mile away and said she was well-acquainted with the Lunneys, having known Ellen for fourteen years. Mrs. Mindrup also was a teacher.

"Her character is good. She is a modest, retiring girl. I never heard a word of censure or suspicion cast against Ellen," Mrs. Mindrup said.

~

Next came Mrs. D. H. Thuma, wife of the justice of the peace Squire Thuma. She lived nearby, three miles west of Lenora and had known Ellen since she attended school with the Thuma's daughter in 1888.

"I was at the Lunneys after the outrage was committed," Mrs. Thuma said. "My husband went with me. We saw Ellen but did not talk to her. She came into the room and her face was very red and swollen as if she had been crying. It looked as though she was in trouble. My husband said he wanted to talk to her and her father. I left the room and went out into the kitchen. I talked with Mrs. Lunney at that time.

"Ellen is as fine a young lady as there is in the neighborhood, and I have never heard a harmful word said against her," Mrs. Thuma said.

~

John Gilleece, a member of a family that was close to both the Lunneys and McEnroes, was called. Gilleece said he knew Gene McEnroe intimately and "associated with him considerable."

How big was Eugene McEnroe?

"I would think he was 135 or 140 pounds," Gilleece said. "He was about my size – heavier if anything. He was stout for his size. He was quick and active. I have wrestled with him. He was the better man, and I claim to be as good as most men my size."

On cross examination, Gilleece said he was a cousin of the defendant. Gilleece was asked about Eugene McEnroe's health.

"On the 24th of July, Gene was in good health. He was in the habit of wearing a mustache but had it shaved off after the rape," Gilleece said.

∾

Enoch Teal said he knew Ellen Lunney. She had taught school in his district.

"She went by my house every day," Teal said. "I never heard anything against her. My children attended school to her. She was modest appearing whenever I saw her."

∾

James Noone, who lived in Graham County, said he knew Eugene McEnroe about five years and "associated with him considerable." Noone would "judge Gene's weight at 135 or 140 pounds. I took him to be tolerable stout for his size. He was active. I weigh from 160 to 165 and he was as good a man as I.

"In the summer of '93 I wrestled with him. My weight was about 145 pounds. We were scuffling on the baseball grounds. Gene generally held his own with all the boys," Noone said.

∾

Elijah H. Darnell, the Lenora constable and former Lenora school board member who testified for the state, was recalled. He described the night of July 24 as "a clear night. I was sleeping out-of-doors. It was a bright, moonlit night." He added that he had known Ellen Lunney for eighteen years and "her character is good."

A neat trick by the defense, calling a prosecution witnesses who would turn out to be a character witness for Ellen.

∾

Horace Russ, who had lived in Lenora township for eleven years, had "stopped there in '89 for twice-a-week for three months."

Why Russ was stopping regularly and staying over at the house was not recorded.

"I know the house they live in. I slept upstairs in the room at the east end of the house. It was a good light room from the east. The bed was in the southwest corner of the room. The window was in the center. When the moon was in the east I could discern objects in that room. I could have recognized anyone. I could see the corn crib plainly.

"I know Ellen. I know her reputation. It is first class," he said.

~

Sarah McKenna, the sister of Anna Lunney, was called to tell of the Lunneys' trip of July 24 that turned into an overnight visit. The Lunney family left for home about eight o'clock the following morning. Mrs. McKenna said she heard reports two days later that Ellen had "been outraged." She saw Ellen the following Sunday at their home. Mrs. Lunney had sent her a note requesting that she come to the Lunneys' home.

She testified: "I saw Ellen on that Sunday. She appeared to be in great distress or trial. She looked very pale. I met her mother first. Ellen did not meet me as usual. She came from the kitchen soon and greeted me. She turned her back to me and cried. I felt so bad for her distress that I went into another room. When I talked to her again I said I was sorry she did not come with her folks, but she said she had to take care of the milk and work. Then we went upstairs. I told the girl not to cry because it was no disgrace. She said, 'Why Aunt Sarah, I would rather he had cut my throat as to do what he did.'"

With the powerful testimony of Sarah McKenna, the court adjourned for the weekend. The defense had run through many of its key witnesses – Ellen Lunney and a large group of character witnesses.

The prosecution had to be worried about the long parade of character witnesses who praised Ellen and her sterling reputation. The prosecution had done little to derail the defense attorneys as their case for justifiable homicide or temporary madness seemed to grow stronger.

The Colonel and Ledru Wilder believed they remained in a strong position, however. They would respond with more questions to a group of witnesses of their own – the McEnroes. Here was a family who had lost a son, a young man who they believed did not deserve to be killed even if he did what Ellen Lunney claimed. The McEnroes would be heard from and the prosecution believed that Gene's father, brothers and sister should be every bit as sympathetic as anyone testifying in the trial.

Next week. That would be when the case would reach its climax.

Twelve

The court reconvened on Monday, and both sets of attorneys appeared rested and ready to continue their intense fight. The prosecution had plenty of cross examination ahead. If the canard were true about the longer the trial the better the chances for the defense, Clinton Angevine and Lafe Thompson had more to gain from extending the length of the event.

Interest in the case had waned, which was unfortunate because the defense soon would call John McKeniff to the witness stand.

"When court was called on Monday, it was apparent that interest in the case, so far as the public is concerned, was dying out. But few people were in the room and for the first time during the trial had there been like even a pretense to orderly quietness," said the *Courier*.

~

Testimony about Ellen's character was not finished. The defense called its first witness of the week, Joshua Wright. He said Ellen Lunney had boarded at his house in Norton while attending school.

"Her actions became a lady at all times," said Wright.

~

Sol Peak, husband of Catherine, an earlier witness for both the prosecution and defense, said he had known the Lunney family for over twenty years "and knew Ellen as well as could be. I've known her since she was born."

Peak was outside Thuma School the day Eugene McEnroe was killed. Peak, an old buffalo hunter, had lived in the Lenora and New Almelo community since he retired from hunting bison and a later career as a farmer. A Civil War veteran who fought for the Second Iowa Infantry, the regiment of future populist leader General James B. Weaver, Peak had been a close neighbor of the Lunneys since he settled along the Solomon. Peak had left occasionally to follow the buffalo hunt on the Nebraska, Colorado and Kansas plains until the animals became scarce in 1876 when he returned to Norton County and became a full-time farmer.

"I saw the Lunneys drive up from Thuma's to the northeast side the day of the shooting. They got out there. The women went right into the school house. I saw them all the time until they went into the school. No one spoke to them. Ellen had a rather pale appearance, white streaks down the side of her nose to her mouth. I had heard her eyes were bloodshot and was otherwise broken down, and I looked especially to see. She is rather of a modest, quiet turn and never speaks unless she is spoken to. She is what I would term a backward girl, never putting herself forward," he said.

The prosecution cross-examined and determined Peak's more precise location outside the school. The defense, on redirect, asked if John McKeniff was there and whether Peak had a conversation with him.

"I saw McKeniff there," said Peak. "I did not speak to him."

$\sim$

The next witness was Nick Dittlinger, who had more to say than to comment on Ellen Lunney's sterling character.

"I know John Lunney, Ellen Lunney, John McKeniff and Eugene and Patsey McEnroe," said Dittlinger.

"I talked with Patsey about it. I think it was on the 27th or 28th of July. It was at my stable. There was no one there but me and him. I said, I did not see how Gene could force Ellen that way, and he said the damn whore did not need forcing, that McKeniff had been using her for six months.

"I don't think we talked any more about it then. I told Will Dunlap about it on Monday the thirtieth at Rockwell's corn crib. I told Dunlap what Patsey had said."

The *Norton Courier* added: "The witness did not testify to the exact words used by Patsey because he said it was not fit to repeat in such a crowd of people."

~

The next witness called was William Dunlap, brother of Anna Lunney.

"My brother married a McEnroe girl. I know Nick Dittlinger. I know John McKeniff. I saw Dittlinger on Monday the 30th day of July at Rockwell's corn crib. We were propping a crib close to the road. He drove up and stopped his team and got to talking to us about the Lunney case. Dittlinger asked me if I was going to listen to the trial. He went on to tell me that Patsey McEnroe told him that Ellen Lunney was a whore and that McKeniff had been using her for the past six months. I do not testify as to the exact words. I would hate to before this crowd.

" I saw McKeniff the same evening coming home from Lenora. I went to Lenora and went to Leonard's Hardware and then got on my horse and started home. McKeniff caught up with me and we rode home together. He asked me if I had heard about Gene raping Ellen Lunney. I told him I had and we conversed about it. I finally told him what Dittlinger had told me in the morning. I told him that Patsey McEnroe had said that Ellen Lunney was a whore and that he (McKeniff) had been using her for six months. McKeniff felt terrible bad at the report. He almost cried. I felt sorry for him," Dunlap said.

~

The next witness was John McKeniff, who said he was Ireland-born and twenty-five years old. Like most of the Irish emigrants to other countries, he was uneducated. The English prohibited the young Irish from learning how to read and write, an attempt at servitude that not always succeeded. There is no indication that John McKeniff had received any sort of an education to learn to read or write or that he tried to gain these skills in the United States.

John McKeniff would be portrayed as a gawky Irish lad, but in fact he stood tall, nearly six feet, and his lanky appearance was not unappealing. His hair and moustache were dark. His dark eyes looked directly at his questioner.

"I have been six years in this country. I came to my uncle's, John Lunney. He paid my way to this country. My brother Hugh came with me. Uncle paid his way, too. I lived at uncle's house for about a year. I lived there after I came and have been there off and on. I call it my home. I had worked around some and then went to work for myself. I worked for Peak and Teal. I farmed land in '94 in Lenora township and boarded at Peak's," said the young man, who must have been worried that he needed to present himself well.

His brother Hugh had met the challenge of moving from Ireland's County Cavan, with its green hills and large, land-holding proprietors, to the middle of the United States where the fields turned brown by July but were more hospitable to the small homesteader. Kansas presented great opportunities in the 1890s with some marginal lands still available for homesteading, and Hugh, among that class of strong, enterprising and hardworking immigrants, seized what he could. Hugh would prosper in his new country. His brother John, the younger, the weaker of the two boys, could not adapt as easily as his brother Hugh. He eventually moved in with the Lunneys, whose crowded three-bedroom house now had to find room for cousin John. He probably would have slept with his younger cousins Tom and Will, forging strong relationships with both but cluttering the Lunney home and dinner table with an unneeded body.

John McKeniff was, in fact, a perfect foil, a young person whose future seemed at the time to be as a hired man when he could find the employment and, because he couldn't keep secret his affection for young Ellen Lunney, someone the prosecution could point to as her possible rapist. Sometimes John McKeniff could be found at the Lunney home; other times one should look for him at his brother's sod shanty. McKeniff continued:

> My brother has a homestead. I have no land. His land is about a mile
> south of the river. He has a sod house in a draw and there is a hill between
> him so we can't see the Lunney's house from there. I made my home with

A photo of John McKeniff, in the late 1890s, shows a dapper, healthy youth. He and his brother Hugh were sons of Catherine McKeniff of County Cavan, Ireland, a sister of John Lunney. John Lunney paid the transportation costs to bring the two McKeniff boys to the United States. (Photo courtesy of Caryl Finnerty.)

him after it got so dry I couldn't farm and couldn't afford to pay board. My brother Hugh and I batched together. Prior to the 24th of July, I was stopping with my brother. I was putting up a pasture fence to put my horses in. I have frequently visited the Lunneys but I was not there on the 24th of July. I had been there the Sunday before the 24th.

I was down on the Solomon River. "It was southeast of Lunney's. I saw Ellen and Mary and the Lunney boys and McEnroe girls and boys. A lot of young people were there. They had a swing. Tom was not there, and it was him who I wanted to see. I did not stop. This was on the 24th of July last.

In his mid-twenties, John McKeniff was too old to be hanging on a swing along the Solomon River. So he pushed his horse along and kept riding.

I heard of a rape being committed on Ellen the day after. I was in Lenora in the forenoon. I returned about sundown. I met E. F. Coleman southeast of the Lunneys' place. You would not pass the Lunney's place in going to my place or going to Lenora. Coleman asked the road to Lunneys and I told him. I went to my brother's. He was in Kansas City. I was alone. I slept outside, sometimes in the wagon and sometimes by it. I had a pair of blankets to sleep on.

John McKeniff slept alone the night of the rape. The prosecution would have questions to ask him about that.
"John Lunney?"

I do not know where he was that day. I did not know he was going on a visit. I heard it the next morning.

I got up the next morning a little after sunup and got breakfast. I took my bed up and threw it in the wagon. It took me a half hour or such to get breakfast. I cooked some meat and coffee. After breakfast I went up to see if the horses were all right. I went to Regester's to get water. I saw Regester and Huffman and had a talk with Huffman about a casting I had lost off his lister. I offered to pay him for it, but he wanted me to order the part.

I went back home. Will Lunney was there when I got back. Regester saw him and told me there was a boy at my place. He thought it was a Lunney boy. It was Will. I whistled to him. He waved his hat to me. Will told me Gene McEnroe had got into the house and raised the dickens. He didn't say what Gene came for. I went back with him. It was about half past eight. John Lunney was not home. He came, I should judge, in some five or ten minutes. I saw him coming when I was going over. The rape was talked over.

I was in Lenora the Thursday after that night. I had a talk with Sy Larrick about the occurrence at the Lunney home. I stopped the greater part of the rest of the week with my uncle John Lunney. Tom went with me to Lenora. I was in Leonard's store. Floyd Richmond clerks in the store. I saw him that day. I went to order a casting for Huffman's lister. I ordered it and did no other business with him. Richmond came from behind the counter and asked if I wanted anything. Then we went to the back room to see a casting and to get the number.

When we went back, Tom asked me to help him buy a revolver. He got a revolver from the show case and asked the price. Richmond said the price was $5.50. It did not suit us so he took it back to the show case and got another. I was in the office when he changed the revolver. The second one was $4.50. After I got the revolver, I put it in my pocket and went out of the store.

I did no other business. After I bought the revolver I went out of the store.

I went home with Tom and stayed there all night. I loaded the revolver, and Tom and I went down the creek and shot it off at a mark. I shot two times and Tom three times. I gave it to Tom and never shot it off again.

The questioning of McKeniff then turned to the day of the shooting at the school.

I was at the school house on July 31st. I went in an old spring wagon. It was an old rattletrap of a wagon, and it had not been used for a year. I had to drive wedges in to keep the tires on. One horse was mine and the other Lunney's. One horse weighed 900 pounds and the other 800 pounds. It was just an ordinary team. Tom went with me. There was but one seat. Mr. and Mrs. Lunney and Ellen went in a lumber wagon about half an hour before we left. Willie went on horseback. We went to Squire Thumas's house first. Will and Squire Thuma rode in my wagon to the school house.

Tom went over to Thuma School to see if the county attorney had come. The Lunneys came behind us, maybe sixty rods behind us. I hitched my team to a post in front of the school house. I was the last in going over, except for the Lunneys. They started ahead of me and I passed them on the road. After I hitched the team, I walked to the door and looked in. This was before the Lunneys came. I did not notice them drive up. I was southeast of the school house. I don't remember seeing them before they went in. I did not speak to them. I went there to hear the trial.

I went to the door to see if the county attorney had come. I was outside when the shooting occurred. I had no talk with Tom or Willie or any of the Lunneys before the shooting. I heard the shooting when I was outside.

> There might have been twenty people outside. We all heard the shooting. We all started for the door. I got a little ways inside the door. I helped Ellen to the wagon.

Did he plan to flee with Ellen?

"I was not going to run away. Never thought of it. I don't remember saying a word. I didn't hear anything said. Her mother was with her and her father was close by."

Where was McKeniff? In the wagon?

"I didn't get into the wagon," McKeniff protested.

The prosecution asked him about the conversation he had with Will Dunlap on the Monday before the shooting.

"I saw him at Lenora. He was on horseback. I rode home with him and he told me that Nick Dittlinger told him that Patsey McEnroe told him that Ellen was a God Damn whore and I had been using her for six months. I felt bad and told Mrs. Lunney about it," he said.

McKeniff said he did not have much experience with firearms.

"I have shot a gun off often, but I don't remember using a revolver for six months prior to this event. Tom told me he wanted me to help him buy a revolver. I was leaning on the show case at the time. I went around and took the one out he pointed to. I took it out and he and I went back to where Floyd Richmond was and we all looked at it. He took it out of my hand and looked at it and snapped it. I asked about the price and Floyd said it was $5.50.

"I never had a conversation with Ellen about practicing with that revolver. I never owned a revolver. I used a revolver of McEnroe's once and one belonging to George Parker. That is all. I don't know if the revolver was loaded after we shot it off down by the river."

Where was McKeniff when the shooting occurred?

"I was about twenty or thirty steps southeast of the school house when I heard the shots. There were other parties outside at the time. There might have been fifteen or twenty people somewhat nearer to the school than I was. I heard someone say that the girl was shooting or that the girl shot him. Some of the others started for the door. I don't know that all of them did," McKeniff said, concluding his testimony.

146

Wilder asked about the gun. Did McKeniff pay for it?

McKeniff replied that Tom paid for it. Why was McKeniff along on the trip to the hardware store? Tom had asked McKeniff to go and help him decide on a gun to buy.

Wilder asked McKeniff again where he was the night of the rape. Sleeping alone by his wagon, he said. Wilder already knew the answer, but he wanted to hear McKeniff say once again that he was alone, just down the draw and over the hill from the Lunneys. Wilder asked if McKeniff knew if anyone saw him at his wagon on the night of the rape.

"No," said McKeniff.

~

Mrs. Anna Lunney, mother of Ellen, was next to be called by the defense.

"I was born in Canada and have been in this country about twenty-three years. I am of Irish descent. My husband was born in Ireland," Anna told the jury.

She was asked several questions about Ellen.

All her lifetime Ella has been industrious with the work about the house and at school. Ellen has always been willing to help about the house. She has always studied hard. Even when she was a little girl, she would not go to bed until she got her lessons done. She would even ask the hired men to help her. My education is not very good. Neither is my husband's, and we could not help her very much. She was always quiet and never cared much to join in with company. She was always very timid, even more so than the smaller children. Her disposition was very retiring.

To my knowledge, she never went to a dance or entertainment without asking me or seeking consent of her brothers. She never cared to go anywhere unless accompanied by her brothers or sisters or her cousins John or Hugh.

Mr. Lunney sent for the McKeniff brothers to come over to this country. John McKeniff or his brother never took her anywhere without my consent. We looked upon them as our own children and treated them as belonging to the family. Ellen has had young men ask her to go places but she always found some excuse not to go.

Mrs. McEnroe died nine years ago. From that time her children were at our house a great deal. They continued to come right along up to the time of the 'trouble.' The boys were there a great deal with our boys.

147

Anna Lunney was asked about the overnight trip to see her relatives, the McKenna family.

> I went with my husband on a visit to my sister's. We intended to come back that night. We went on Tuesday but did not return that evening. My sister coaxed me to stay and we did.
>
> We left the next morning for home and got there about nine o'clock. Tom and Willie came out of the house crying. They could not tell us what the matter was. Willie said, "Father, you will find out soon enough." In a while Mr. Lunney called us upstairs and told us about it.
>
> Ellen said it was pain that woke her up. The quilt was on the other side of the bed, and there was a lot of plaster on the bed. The next morning she said her arms and legs were all sore. She said, "Oh mother, you don't know what I've gone through." She showed me her knees and they were all sore.
>
> Mr. Lunney and Ellen started off to get Gene arrested. Ellen was crying all the time. She didn't scarcely eat anything and didn't want to show herself to the other children. The longer she thought of it the worse she seemed to feel. She did considerable praying. I saw her on her knees two or three times a day, praying for God to direct her what was best to do. I used to tell her not to feel so bad but she answered each time, "I would rather he had killed me." She said she could take her own life for she had nothing to live for now. She frequently said she wished she could die, that all she had to live for was over. She did not feel like eating or sleeping.

One can almost hear the silence that must have pervaded the courtroom. Eyes down, perhaps tugging a little at her dress or twisting a handkerchief in her hands as Anna struggled to get the words out. Her oldest daughter raped while she and her husband were off visiting her sister and her family, having a good time instead of being home to protect her daughter. The guilt would have been overwhelming, choking her.

It is hard to say how well-equipped she was to deal with such a tragedy. Certainly, the Victorian era strictures of the time did not allow families to discuss such things openly. Better to hide such things and pretend they did not exist rather than discuss them and shed the light of day on them. As any mother, her heart must have ached to help as she watched her daughter Ellen deal with her depression, hearing how she would rather be dead than raped.

And then comes the shooting and the destruction she saw it

bringing to her entire family. How completely and utterly dreadful it must have been. And now she had to recount all this to a judge and twelve men she did not know. It must have been nearly more than Anna Lunney could bear.

"I told her she could not help what had happened. She would have to bear it patiently. She usually slept very sound but after this occurred, she would jump at the least sound if I went upstairs."

Anna Lunney was asked to relate what John McKeniff had told her on July 30.

> I talked with McKeniff about reports about Ellie. He told me that Bill Dunlap told him what he heard Patsey McEnroe told Nick Dittlinger that Ellie was a bad girl and that John had been going with her for six months. I told Ellie about it. We were at the well and we sat down. I told her the same as what John McKeniff had told me. She asked and I told her that Patsey had told it to her uncle. She cried and said, "Why do they tell such lies."

The questioning shifted to the day of the shooting.

"I was at the school house the thirty-first of July. I went with Mr. Lunney and Ellie. We started quite early. We went in a lumber wagon. It is not very new. It had one seat," she said.

Mrs. Lunney was asked about seeing John McKeniff at Thuma School.

"McKeniff stayed at our house the remainder of the week after the rape. He was sick. I next saw him at Thuma's. I don't recall talking to him. I next saw him when Ellie and I were in the buggy after the shooting occurred.

"I had my veil on," Mrs. Lunney said. "I don't recall seeing John pass us when we went to the school."

> We got out of the wagon and walked right into the school house. I did not speak to anyone or anyone to us. No one spoke to Ellie. Ellie was on the left side of me. I don't remember stopping. When I walked in, I looked for a seat. I didn't notice a vacant seat. I saw Gene McEnroe. I couldn't tell what Ellie was doing.
>
> I heard two or three shots. I didn't know what it was. I didn't know Ellie had a revolver. I saw them all gathered around. I can't say I saw a revolver in her hand. I saw one in Darnell's. I took hold of Ellie. I guess Regester

was there. There was such a crowd and confusion. There were a good many people in the schoolroom. I was not aware of our separation, if there was one, after the shooting. I went out as soon as I could get out. Ellie went out before me. I followed along after her. We went south of the schoolhouse and got into the buggy. McKeniff did not get into the buggy.

This testimony did not give much help to the prosecution, who contended that Ellen planned to flee with McKeniff and her brother Tom. If McKeniff did not climb into the buggy, he must not have planned to run away with Ellen. Even the family's own lawyers kept asking a lot of questions about McKeniff. Was that poor, gangly boy that much of a suspect or did the prosecution merely want to take advantage of his vulnerability?

"Ellen has not been home since that morning. Ellen's monthly period had been regular up to that time. She had her monthly on the 25th of July. She did not show me her drawers. I took them while she was gone with her father to have Gene arrested. They were stained from her monthly. I could not tell whether this was caused by Gene's act," she said.

"I did not think when I put them to soak that they would be material in this case," Mrs. Lunney replied to a question why she washed what would have been important evidence.

Washing Ellen's drawers eliminated evidence about a rape and, in addition, information about her period.

The Colonel cross-examined Anna Lunney, and the prosecutor pressed her hard for answers.

"That was the first time we ever went away visiting and left Ella alone," Mrs. Lunney said in reply to Jones' question.

Why did Mrs. Lunney tell Ellen about the reports supposedly circulating about her? Wouldn't that upset her daughter even more?

"I was solicitous about her peace, but I had to tell her what the McEnroes told about her so she would know what she had to expect," Mrs. Lunney said. "She was feeling worse before this and wanted to kill herself. I told her two reports I had heard."

And the pistol, in the house for several days? She did not know anything about another gun being in the house, or that her daughter was practicing shooting it down by the river?

"I did not know there was a new revolver that had been bought or that one other than Mr. Lunney's was in the drawer," she said.

"Did Ella wear a veil to the schoolhouse? I don't know whether or not Ella wore a veil to the schoolhouse. I wore one. She wore a cloak.

> As soon as we alighted, Ella and I went into the schoolhouse. After we entered I did not notice Ella. I saw Eugene as I entered the door. He looked at us grinning and laughing. I walked in with her and expected to sit by her. I was looking to the east for a seat for both of us.
>
> I don't remember what I did after the first firing. The shots were quick, and the men were jumping up and around. I was so excited I did not know what had happened. I can scarcely tell you how I got out of doors. I was following Ella.
>
> When we got into the buggy she said: "Mamma, where were you. I did not know what had happened to you."

The questioning then referred to the rape.

"Next morning after the rape I saw blood on the sheet and on the pillow, round spots about as large as the palm of the hand," Mrs. Lunney said.

Didn't she tell a Mr. Bradbury, who was at the house with her brother, William Dunlap, that blood had come from Ella's nose?

"No. I did not state to Bradbury that Eugene placed his hand so forcibly over Ella's mouth as to press against her nose and make it bleed. I did not say to him the bed was in the same condition as when the rape occurred. The girls slept in it after the rape," she said.

Jones ended his questioning. He had been rough, probing Anna with prying questions and trying to force her into a mistake. He failed, and Anna seemed a sympathetic witness who had been bullied by powerful prosecutors.

"I don't know what Mr. Jones meant when he asked me if I regained consciousness when I got into the wagon," Mrs. Lunney said in answer to a question on redirect from Clint Angevine. "I wasn't unconscious. I was so excited I really didn't know what I was doing."

Mrs. Lunney stepped down from the witness stand.

Thirteen

The defense next called Tom Lunney, the seventeen-year-old brother of Ellen Lunney who had been charged as an accessory. Young Tom was outgoing, learning the responsibility of manhood but still a teenager who spent time with youngsters near his age. Where was he on the day of the rape?

"On Tuesday, July 24, I was at home part of the forenoon. I saw Dan, Patsey and Gene," Tom Lunney said.

> Gene and Patsey were cutting corn. Dan wasn't doing anything. I cut a round or so with Patsey in the afternoon. Towards evening Dan came and took supper at our house. Patsey came after supper, about sundown. We had intended to go down to Taylor's to take a bath in the river, but we didn't go. Coleman came soon after. He was not in the house. After Coleman went away we went to the house to get the pails to do the milking.
>
> Father and mother left home about eight or nine in the morning. I said to Ellie that I didn't believe the folks would come home that night. The McEnroe boys were there with me. After we got the pails and did the milking, me and Patsey went after apples. It was close to nine o'clock. We went afoot. We were gone about one and a half hours. We got some apples and then came back.
>
> I can't say whether the moon was up or not. We went to the granary and found Dan and Willie on the bed. They got up, talked and ate the apples. We stayed maybe fifteen minutes and then Dan and Patsey went home. I went to the well and got a drink and went to bed. I did not see Ellen after we came back from getting the apples. There was no light in the house. We were used to sleeping in the granary.
>
> I was awakened by Ellen's hollering. I got up and she told me that Gene McEnroe was in the house. I asked if he was still there. She said no and pointed to the direction he had gone.
>
> I went to the house and got father's revolver. I went down past the crib to the creek. I shot it off twice. I don't know how quick it might have been.

It might have taken a couple of minutes. I called the dog and hollered "sic! sic!" I went in the direction Ellen pointed.

The bank south of the house is twelve to fifteen feet high. The ground to the creek is nearly level. It is sixty or seventy yards to the head of the slope. There is a small draw between our house and McEnroe's. It is about one-half or a fourth of a mile from our house to the McEnroes to the southwest. The draw is a small one and you couldn't see anyone in it from our house.

After I fired the shots I did not return for about ten minutes. I went to the granary because Ellie and Willie were there. They were standing, I think, in the granary. I must have been fifteen or twenty yards away from them. I don't remember whether we said anything or not. There was no light in the house. We went into the house. Ellie told me what Gene had done.

It was a light night. I never took particular notice of where the moon was. I could distinguish a person from one hundred yards. I don't know what quarter of the moon it was.

When we went into the house we lit the lantern. Ellie said it was twenty minutes to one. It was light in the room. When we put out the light we could see to distinguish objects. The moon shown in. I stayed in the upstairs west room the rest of the night.

When I got up the next morning the sun was up. After breakfast I went to where one of the McEnroe's was cutting corn. It was Patsey. I went out to where Patsey was at work. When I went up to him, he said "hello." I answered back. I asked him, "Was Gene at home when he got back last night?" He said "yes, he was at home, in bed asleep."

The two boys had gone as close friends into the night's darkness to steal crab apples from a neighbor. But that friendship had ruptured in the stillness of the dark. Tom had spent ten minutes, armed with a family revolver, searching the riverbank with the dogs. He may have gone close to the McEnroe home to see if anyone was stirring. But that is not recorded.

Tom and Patsey never again would be close friends.

After I came back Willie went over to the McKeniff's place. He started over there pretty early in the morning. John McKeniff came back with him. Father and mother arrived in about fifteen minutes after John came. I went out to the wagon when they drove up. Ellie was in the house. Father asked how we were getting along. I didn't say anything. I commenced unhitching the horses. There was talk of what had happened. We talked

about having Gene arrested. I did not go with them when they went to
have Gene arrested.

He was shown photographs of the Lunney farmyard. He
described areas of the yard, pointed out where the granary was
located and where he went to shoot the revolver.

When Ellen came to the granary, she was excited and hollering. I
understood in a general way from her appearance and what she said what
had happened. The ceiling above Ellen's bed comes within about a foot of
the bed. When the bed is shoved back as far as it will go, the roof or ceiling
is about one foot from it. The bed was shoved back as close as it could be
against the wall. The bed was standing in its usual position.

I talked with Willie about going after John McKeniff. We were in the
granary lying on the bed. I saw Dan McEnroe after I saw Patsey. About ten
or fifteen minutes later Dan came to the door and I saw him. He said hello
and I said hello. Willie was lying with his face down. I asked Dan if Gene
came home from the divide last night and he said yes. "He slept with
Johnny last night." Willie left the granary while Dan was there and went to
McKeniff's place. There was not very much conversation between Dan
and I. He only stayed a short time. He did not make known any special
business. He went home. It was early in the morning when he made his
first visit. It must have been between seven and eight o'clock.

After he left this time I saw him again in an hour or an hour and a half
down at the stable. He came from down the creek. He came from their
place. He had no errand that I know of. I did not talk to him at all. I don't
know the exact time of the second visit. It was in the forenoon sometime. I
did not see him talking to anyone at that time. He was around about the
stable and the granary.

Dan seems to have been doing a little barnyard snooping, a
vanguard from the McEnroe home to see how the Lunneys were
handling their problem.

The questioning moved to buying Ellen a revolver.

On Thursday the 26th of July last, me and John were going to town and
when we were ready Ellen came to me and asked to get her a revolver. She
had talked with me in the morning about it. She wanted to get father's
revolver and learn her how to shoot. I told her it was hard to pull off.

We went to town in the afternoon. When we went to Leonard's Hardware Store, John asked Floyd Richmond about a casting. Floyd went to the
back part of the store. I asked John to buy me a revolver and to get one out

of the show case. We took it back to where Floyd was and asked the price of it. It did not suit us and we looked at another one and bought it.

We had never talked of buying it before nor was there any talk of it. I got the money from father's pocket. I was in the habit of getting money this way when I wanted it. I had this privilege nearly as long as I can remember.

A young man buying a revolver for $4.50, not a small sum when money was in short supply, and taking the money from his father's pocket for the purchase? John McKeniff had testified that he had bought the pistol, but the Lunney family's money had paid for it. The jurors may have wondered how much wealth John Lunney possessed to have been carrying $4.50 in his pocket around the farmyard. The Norton County sheriff routinely foreclosed on farms that could not pay a few hundred dollars in debt. Or did John Lunney simply give his son the money?

John carried the revolver home. We went down to the creek that evening and shot at a tree. Five shots were fired. John shot two and I shot the other three. He gave me the revolver and cartridges and I put them in my pocket.

I loaded it again and put it in the drawer of a safe – a clothes safe. It was something we kept clothes in. I saw the revolver the next evening. I took it out of the drawer and put it in my pocket and I and Ellen went out and practiced. We went down to the timber and Ellen shot five times at a tree which was a foot through. Anyway, she was about two steps from it and she hit the root of the tree once. When she would shoot she would whirl her head around and shoot. She did not see what she was shooting.

I laughed at her. The revolver I purchased is easier to shoot than father's. I don't know if she practiced any other time. I reloaded the revolver and took it up and put it in the drawer. She never used the revolver or shot it off until at the schoolhouse. This is the first time I know of Ellen using firearms.

I was at Thuma's. I went in a buggy with McKeniff. It was an old rickety buggy which had been standing under the shed and had not been used for a year because the tires were loose. We had to put wedges under the tires to keep them on. We drove a horse team. It was an ordinary team. I was at Thuma's, I don't know how long. I went to the schoolhouse on horseback. I took the horse Will had rode to Thuma's. I went at father's request to see if the lawyers had come. The crowd was just about there when I got there. I went because father told me to go. The McEnroes went before I did.

There was lots there that I couldn't name. I was there when father, mother and Ellen came. I saw McKeniff, Will and Squire Thuma come together. McKeniff had been there only a short time before father came. Father drove to the northeast corner of the schoolhouse. I saw their wagon stop. Ellen and mother got out right away and started right in. Nobody talked to them before they went in.

I did not go in before the shooting. I was inquiring if the lawyers had got there when the shooting occurred. I was at the front of the schoolhouse shortly. Prior, I saw McKeniff around the schoolhouse. The minute I heard the shooting I rushed in. All the people rushed in. I did not see McKeniff. Ellen was standing between the center part of the house toward the south. Patsey had his hands over her shoulders. I grabbed him by the collar to jerk him loose.

Ellen got out before I did. When I got out and I saw her next, she was going toward the wagon. McKeniff, Mother and Father were close to her. I saw them near the wagon. Ellen and her mother got into the seat. I did not see anyone else in the wagon.

Since that day I have been in the jail most of the time.

Again, another question about buying the revolver.

"When Ellen asked me to buy her a revolver she did not say what she wanted to do with it," Tom Lunney said.

His testimony did not do much to strengthen the defense's case. Not only did Tom supposedly take the money from his father's pants pocket, but his father apparently did not notice or ask about the loss of his money. Nor did Tom ask his sister what she intended to do with the weapon. He also revealed that she was standing a few steps from the tree that served as a target. Did she believe that any attacker would be close to her or that any intended target would be only steps away. Or perhaps it was Ellen who intended to be only a few feet away?

The colonel cross-examined Tom and asked questions to clear up several questions, including the relationship with the McEnroe boys.

"Dan had been accustomed to calling at our place. We received him well. The best of terms existed between us. When Dan came this time (the day after Ellen's rape), he did not say much like he used to."

The colonel inquired about what else Tom did in Lenora the day he bought the gun.

"John McKeniff and I went to Lenora, I for the mail, John for the casting. Before going into the hardware store, I had been into Richmond's, into Barbo's and the post office," Tom said in mentioning businesses in Lenora.

"I had no business in these other places."

And buying the revolver at the hardware store?

"Floyd Richmond was near the door when we entered. McKeniff spoke to him the first thing about the casting. When he was in the back room, I asked John to help me pick out a revolver. He got the one I desired and took it back to Floyd," Tom recounted.

Ellen practiced with the revolver on Friday evening. She did not say why she desired to learn to shoot.

After the others started to Thumas, it may have been an hour and a half before John and I started. I was at Thumas for a while before the crowd left for the schoolhouse.

Ellen practiced with the revolver a half, maybe a quarter of a mile, east. The tree was a foot through. The revolver was about three or four feet from the tree. She shot five times and turned her head away every time.

She did not say anything about being a poor shot or that she needed a lot of practice. Ellen was not present after I loaded the revolver after that at the house.

The six-shot revolver would have been loaded with five shells for safety, meaning that inexperienced Ellen emptied the pistol when she practiced and when she shot Gene McEnroe.

"When I rushed into the schoolhouse, I did not know what had happened. I pulled him away," he said of Patsey McEnroe, "because I did not want him to have hold of my sister. He did not look right. He was rough with her. He said nothing. Nobody said what happened.

"She was out of the school by the time I let go of Patsey. Then I went to the buggy, to the heads of the horses. John McKeniff was there.

"I got into the schoolhouse after the shots. I did not see my mother or McKeniff when I entered," Tom Lunney said as his cross examination ended.

∾

Next on the witness stand was Will Lunney, fifteen-year-old brother of Ellen, who was asked about the events of Tuesday, July 24. Will, a quiet youth who kept to himself, spent more time than his brother Tom or his younger brother Jack fishing, hunting and wandering along the river. Will was the same age as Patsey, but it seemed that Tom had been a closer friend with the McEnroe youth. Like his sister Ellen, Will was shy, sensitive and introspective. He didn't seem to mind walking in Tom's shadow.

"I saw Dan, Patsey and Gene McEnroe that day (the day after the rape). They were cutting fodder southeast of our house. Gene had his mustache cut off and his face shaved clean. He wore a mustache two or three weeks before that. On that day he was clean shaven."

The day of the rape?

> I first saw Dan at their house about nine o'clock. I went over to see if he was at home and stayed till noon. We went to where they were cutting fodder and then went back to McEnroe's house. Dan and Patsey were at our house during the evening. Dan ate supper with us, and Patsey came about sundown. We talked around for a while and then I went for the cows.
>
> When I got back, Mr. Coleman had come. He stayed about an hour. He had a stable horse there. We went to milk and Dan helped. We took the milk down in the cellar, and Ellen took care of it. We all had a talk out by the well about the folks coming home that night, and Tom asked Ellen if she thought they would be coming and she said, "If they are coming, they would be here by this time."
>
> After that Pat and Tom went after apples at Leonard's place. Dan and I went into the granary and got into bed. I went to sleep. I woke when the two boys came back from getting apples. I don't know whether Dan slept or not.
>
> I got up and we ate the apples. Then the two McEnroe boys went home. I don't know whether the moon was up or not. I think it was about eleven o'clock. Me and my brother went to the well to get a drink. It was light. I don't think it was cloudy when the boys went away. We went to bed and to sleep.

Will described a lazy summer evening, an outing by his brother and Patsey to steal a few apples, an evening turning into night and the expectation of a normal night's sleep. No one brought forth a farmer's almanac during the trial, but the normal time for sunset in late July in western Kansas was shortly before nine o'clock. If Will is correct that it was about eleven o'clock when they grabbed a cup of water from the well, the sun would have been set long before and the night, truly, must have been bright and lit by the moon.

> I next woke when I heard Ellen holler. She was at the granary door. I got up. Tom was up, too. Tom went to the house to get a pistol and went down southeast past the crib. He went towards the river. Tom went from the house past the crib. Ellen said Gene went that way. He was gone about ten minutes. Ellen stayed with me in the granary. I heard two shots fired in the direction Tom went. When he came back, we went to the house.
>
> We were standing in the granary door. It was light and clear. The moon was up. It was in the southeast. I don't remember if it was full. I could see a person I was acquainted with at seventy-five yards. I could distinctly see a person at the crib. It was sixty or seventy-five yards away.
>
> When we went out of the house we locked the doors and went to bed. I locked the doors. There was a lantern lit and we took it upstairs. Ellen looked at the clock and said it was thirty minutes to one. I stayed upstairs in the west room, and Ellen was in the east room the rest of the night.
>
> There was not much said about Gene being there.
>
> We got up by sunup next morning. Tom got up first. After breakfast I found the screen of the door torn near the latch. We examined it and found the screen torn off right where the door latched on the inside. The wire was torn from the frame. About one half foot torn off.

He was asked to identify the door. Will did, and it was placed in evidence.

The *Champion* noted that, "The jury examined the door with particular care."

Was the intruder Eugene McEnroe?

That was the person Ellen identified, and the person she had identified to her brothers as the man who had raped her.

"It was in this condition when I examined it," Will Lunney said of the screen. "It was taken off about three weeks ago."

> On the morning of the 25th of July last Tom and I talked about getting McKeniff to come and it was decided that I should go. Dan McEnroe

came to our place that day between seven and eight o'clock. Tom and I were in the granary and he was standing at the door. He spoke to Tom and came in. I stayed a couple of minutes and then went to McKeniff's. I did not say anything about going.

We had been crying just before he came. I was gone after McKeniff from a half hour to an hour. He lives a mile from our house. He was over at Regester's, a quarter mile from his house. I stayed about fifteen minutes. He (McKeniff) went home with me.

I went over afoot. When I returned Dan was not there. He came back about about half an hour after we got there, but he did not come to the house. He spoke to McKeniff.

"I don't know of any errand he had there either time. He spoke only to John McKeniff. He stayed about fifteen minutes the second time. I don't know his errand at either time. Father and Ellen left while he was there the second time. They went east toward Lenora while he was there. He left in about five minutes after they did. He went towards home.

The visits of Dan McEnroe must have caused anxiety within the Lunney family. Did Dan come over because he was sent by his older brother Gene or his father to fathom the the feelings of the Lunneys or to learn what they were doing? It must have been difficult for Ellen to have her attacker's brother show up uninvited at the house. Whatever she felt, she kept it to herself. If her father said anything to the young man, no one commented on it. The whole family undoubtedly was stunned and reeling from the night's happenings. Dan would be asked later about his reason for going to the Lunneys.

Willie Lunney was cross examined by Colonel Jones. He said he had lived on the Lunney farm all his life.

"We boys were always friends," he said of the McEnroes. "I did not see Dan with any of our people. He came first to the stable, then to the granary. Dan was nearby when Father and Ellen got in the buggy and drove away. Shortly after this Dan left for home."

I did not see Dan after that, nor Eugene that day.

I went to Thuma's on horseback, and to the schoolhouse in a wagon. I went to the school with McKeniff and Squire Thuma. Tom rode my horse to the school. I was not at the school when the shooting occurred. I was tying the team which Father drove. Before I got to the school, Ellen and Ma were out at the wagon. They drove up to the northeast corner and father unhitched the horses. I was at the team yet when the shooting occurred. I don't know what happened at the schoolhouse or in front of it. After the shooting, about twelve o'clock, I went home.

"On horseback," Will said in concluding his testimony.

Fourteen

Large audiences returned to the Norton County Courthouse as the murder trial again became the main topic of conversation among Norton's merchant class, particularly the wives of the local businessmen. The trial attracted a large number of women observers, who crammed into the small courtroom to watch the most significant trial in Norton County's history. The *Norton Champion* printed a revealing paragraph about the women who had been attracted to the courtroom by stories about a young woman on trial for killing the man who had attacked and raped her in her own bed.

"Some husbands in this city, so we are confidently informed, have subsisted on two meals a day for the last ten days, the morning meal before sunup, the evening meal after nine; their wives were attending court and took along their dinners (the midday meal) in order to secure front seats."

Women may not have been allowed on juries in 1894, but probably many of them bent their husband's ear when they finally got together for supper, the evening meal.

The defense recalled Elijah H. Darnell, the Lenora constable, to help build its case of Ellen Lunney's temporary madness. He had arrested Ellen Lunney at Thuma School House after the shooting.

> I told her she should consider herself under arrest. Her condition at that time mentally and physically seemed peculiar. She did not pay any attention to me at all. She did not notice her arrest at all. When I walked up and put my hand on her and told her that she was under arrest, she paid no attention to me at all and did not appear to realize even that I was an officer.
>
> I laid my hand on her shoulder and told her to consider herself under

163

arrest, but then she seemed indifferent to it and later asked me what I was going to do with her. She looked over her shoulder and there was a very peculiar look in her eyes.

A woman behaving peculiarly. Not resisting arrest at this point since the revolver had been wrested from her but ignoring officer Darnell. Indifferent to what happened around her, except looking for her mother, with a peculiar look in her eyes. Darnell maintained a prominent place in Lenora's community. He not only was a constable picked to uphold the law but had been elected by the voters to serve on the town's school board.

Peculiar. The constable used the word at least twice.

The Lenora constable, who was proving to be an excellent defense witness, was asked about Effie Norlin.

"I know Effie Norlin. I subpoenaed her. She asked me what do they want of me? I said, I suppose that you told Jones something or he would not have subpoenaed you. She was staying at her sister's. She said that Ellen Lunney did not tell her anything about the case," Darnell said, contradicting young Effie's claim that Ellen confided that "if she had to do it over, she would do it again."

Had little Effie told a fib when she testified for the prosecution? Effie is a difficult young lady to analyze. Barely eighteen, she had been a rape victim and more than a casual acquaintance of Ellen Lunney's. She was in protective custody of the sheriff, not because she was charged with any crime, pending the trial of her rapist. Either she contradicted herself when testifying under oath, or Ellen lied about what she had told Effie. Young witnesses often prove unreliable on the witness stand, and Effie was no exception. The defense seemed to be satisfied with Constable Darnell's testimony, which challenged Effie's credibility. But the prosecution wasn't satisfied.

~

First Ellen Lunney was called by the state for further cross examination on a touchy subject. She said that, "After the commission of the rape, I did not submit my private parts to any physician for examination."

164

On recross examination by the defense, Ellen Lunney said that, "Neither the attorney for the state, nor any other person suggested it. Mr. Thompson suggested it after he became my attorney. It was about the third of August.

"I did not know that it was of any importance," the defendant said.

With that testimony, the defense rested its case.

⁓

The state offered rebuttal testimony. The prosecution wanted Effie Norlin back on the witness stand in hopes of undoing some damage from what Constable Darnell had said.

"I had a conversation with Ellen Lunney in reference to the killing of Eugene McEnroe," Effie Norlin said. "It was in the kitchen of the sheriff's house after Ellen was brought there. I asked her if she remembered if she saw plainly whether it was Gene McEnroe. She said she didn't."

There were objections to the testimony for reasons that were unstated by the reporters covering the trial. For whatever reason, the objection was sustained and the jurors told to ignore her statement.

On cross-examination, Effie said she "was on the stand last week and testified to the question as to what Ellen said. I asked her several questions and she did not answer them."

Effie's last answer constituted her final version of conversations with Ellen. Effie asked the questions but Ellen did not respond.

⁓

James McEnroe, the 65-year-old father of Eugene McEnroe, was called to tell his version of the events of the evening of July 24. As the head of the family, he stood as the key person who could establish an alibi for his son Eugene on the night of the rape.

James McEnroe and his family seemed to have fewer good years than bad years on the plains. County records indicate the family farm was nearing foreclosure at the time of the trial. There is no indication the McEnroes boys found work outside the home although they had reached an age when that should have been an option, if jobs could be found. Had the McEnroe boys ever traveled outside the area, perhaps to Denver to see the Rocky Mountains? No one indicated they had.

Young people did travel if they could afford the train ticket. They could go from the midwest to the east or west coasts in a few days by rail. Once the railroad arrived, prosperous young persons could be married and honeymoon in a growing city such as Denver or Kansas City. A Lenora newspaper item in 1886 told of a local merchant, Joseph Barbo, who had taken his three young daughters to South Bridge, Massachusetts, "where they go to school."

Quebec-born Barbo had four daughters by a first marriage before his wife died. His three sons by a later marriage, Guy, Virgil and Ross, became important businessmen in promoting Lenora's growth in the twentieth century. But such travel, even by a prospering businessman, was a little unusual in western Kansas in 1894.

One question for James McEnroe, of course, was the whereabouts of his son on the evening he allegedly spent raping his neighbor Ellen Lunney.

Joe Barbo conducted a successful mercantile business in Lenora. He owned a large amount of property in the town and Lenora's old stone hotel. Barbo built a large Victorian home on the east edge of Lenora's downtown district. (Photo from F. M. Lockard, *The History of the Early Settlement of Norton County, Kansas.*)

I was at home. Eugene was at home that evening. I sent him to the divide five miles from home to look at some fox grass, to see if it was too dead to do anything with. When he came back he went in the house and eat his supper and after supper he read the paper 'till ten o'clock. Then he went to bed in the granary. It was

166

my granary. It is northeast of the house twenty-five or thirty yards from the house. He went to bed.

Patsey and Dan were, I supposed, at the Lunneys. I did not see them come home. I don't know when they did come home. I started to go for them and between my place and Lunney's I got caught in a barbed wire fence. I was some time in getting myself loose. When I did I gave up going and returned to the house. I was at the granary before I started, and Gene and my little boy were there at eleven-thirty. After this I went and got two or three arms full of corn fodder and threw it in to the pigs. I also carried some shelled corn to some pigs I was fattening.

I went to the granary again to see if the boys had got back. They hadn't and I went to bed. I was not awake when they came home. I did not know when they came home until the next morning. I was up the next morning before daylight. I went to the granary to see if the boys had got there. They had.

Jurors tuned closely to the case should have noticed that James McEnroe said he knew exactly where his son Gene was on the night in question but that two younger sons had not arrived home at eleven-thirty. Tom Lunney had testified that he and Patsey had "gone after apples" at close to nine o'clock and returned an hour and a half later. Dan, Patsey, Willie and Tom hung around the Lunney granary another fifteen minutes or so. But James McEnroe's testified that he became tangled in barbed wire and was "sometime getting myself loose." He gave up and returned home and found Gene and a younger son asleep at eleven-thirty.

Where were Dan and Patsey for forty-five minutes? And then old man McEnroe went out and collected three bundles of corn fodder for the pigs at a time that all the jurors knew that it had been dark for two hours, and when he finished young Dan and Patsey still had not arrived home? And, while tangled in the barbed wire, he never called out to son Gene, nearby in the granary, to untangle him from his predicament?

A king-size inconsistency had appeared in the main witness claiming to know where his son Gene spent the night. It would be only the first inconsistent testimony the father would offer.

∾

On cross-examination by defense counsel, James McEnroe was asked if he knew two neighbors, James Donahoe and Frank Organ. He replied that he knew Donahoe and Organ but denied talking to them as the two neighbors claimed.

James Donahoe and Frank Organ, the two neighbors, had said that James McEnroe told them of suspicions about his son Gene being the rapist. McEnroe would deny the conversations took place.

"I saw him (Donahoe) on the day that Eugene was killed and had a talk with him at my house. I know Frank Organ. He was there that night. I have no recollection of talking with Donahoe and Organ that night at the front of my house" (on July 31).

Angevine questioned the elderly man about what other witnesses had said, and the result kept McEnroe on the defensive.

"I don't recollect saying to them that Patsey and Dan were with the Lunney boys and I was afraid that they would go to Dutch Miller's orchard for apples and I was anxious for them for fear they might get a load of shot."

This would have been a realistic fear. Farmers frequently, upon hearing someone stealing fruit such as crab apples or watermelons from their fields, blasted away with a shotgun, often more angered about being awakened than by the loss of their produce. If a young thief received a load of lead in the buttocks, a doctor or someone else always could pick it out. Shotguns fired at a distance were meant to wound superficially or scare the young thieves into leaving.

> I did not say that they came home between ten and eleven o'clock. I did not say to them at that time and place that I knew the Lunneys were away from home. I did not say to them that I went two or three times to the granary, and that Gene was in the granary each time in bed and that the boys got home between ten and eleven o'clock. I never made the statement to James Donahoe or Frank Organ or to anybody that I was afraid that the boys would go to Dutch Miller's to steal apples and get a load of shot.
>
> I did not say to Donahoe or Organ that I had no doubt that someone had disturbed Ellen as she claimed, and that it was either Eugene or John McKeniff.

On the 24th of July, I returned to my home in the afternoon. Gene took his little brother and went to bed. The little boy had a bed of his own. The door stood open all the time. Gene slept in a bed of his own close to the door. I went to bed, I presume it was about twelve o'clock. I went out to see if the boys had come home. I had no other reason to go out.

Gene went to bed at ten. I wasn't in the house all the time. I carried fodder to my hogs about nine or thereabouts. Carried two or three armloads. Carried it about twenty yards. It fed the fattening hogs. It was a little after dark. I don't know how long. I fed them corn, five hogs that I was fattening. I carried it in a bucket. I got the corn in the house and had to carry it thirty or forty yards. It didn't take long. It might have taken me half an hour. I think it did. After I rested a while I cut two or three armloads of green fodder. It took me over two hours to feed the corn and cut it. It took me two hours or three. I carried it fully sixty yards.

It was not a very dark night. The moon was up. No, I am not in the habit of feeding the hogs so late. I could not walk fast. I had rheumatism and was obliged to stop and rest occasionally. It was very painful and must have taken me over two hours. Then I sat down on a chair and rested a half hour. Then I went to the granary to see if the boys had come home. I did not see Dan and Patsey that night. I saw them the next morning and had a conversation with them.

The head of the McEnroe family was proving to be a detriment to the prosecution. Under Angevine's skillful questioning, the old farmer gave different times that he fed the pigs, and readers of the *Champion* newspaper would have wondered how much he said was truthful. He seemed so excited that he could not remember one daughter's age. Angevine had led James McEnroe into spending all his energy in defending the honor of his family and his son Gene. He wanted to portray the family as industrious, so industrious that his daughter Ellen would stay up well into the summer night to mend a winter coat for a young boy. His sons may have been running over to the Lunneys to see their friends or out stealing apples, but James McEnroe would be spending the night carrying fodder to feed his hogs while Eugene slept in the granary. Was James stretching the truth so far that the veracity of his entire family would be questionable in the jurors' minds? Gene McEnroe wasn't the individual on trial; Ellen Lunney was, but the elderly father's priority seemed to be defending his family, not convicting his son's killer.

The name of my eldest daughter at home is Ellen. She is about eighteen. Another daughter – Agnes, she's eight or nine – talked with Ellen that night, when the boys were at Lunneys. I saw Ellen in the kitchen sewing that night at eleven thirty. After Eugene went to bed no one else but Ellen and me were in the kitchen. I told her it was eleven thirty and she ought to go to bed. She said she had to mend some clothes first.

Mending clothes in the middle of the night? Farmers customarily rose early, feeding their hungry hogs and cows who awakened with the sun. Sunrise would have been about six-thirty.

When she went to bed she woke Mary, my little girl. She told her to get up and she undressed her and put her to bed. She told her it was twelve o'clock.

I know James Gilleece. I saw him the day Gene was buried. I don't recollect talking with him or taking him to the granary where the boys slept. It is likely I had a talk with him. I have no recollection of taking him out to the granary to see where the boys slept. It is possible that I might have done so.

Attorney Angevine quizzed the witness closely on the fact that he did all this work of cutting and lugging feed to the hogs while his son Gene, "a strong, active, healthy young man, was lying asleep in his bed."

The *Norton Courier* said that, "The excuse the witness gave for so doing was that he wanted to shame the boys by telling them the next day that by reason of their absence he had to do this work. He said he wanted to jaw them about it."

On recross examination, Colonel Jones asked, "What is the character of Eugene McEnroe?"

Angevine jumped to his feet and objected, saying Eugene's character was no part of the issue before the jury. Judge Geiger sustained his objection. Had Geiger ruled otherwise the door would have opened to an entirely new path – what was the popular Gene McEnroe like?

Why wouldn't Geiger allow such testimony, which certainly would be of interest to the jury? Perhaps he acted as jurists sometimes do, trying to trim some time off the trial that already was becoming lengthy. The prosecution would have been the beneficiary of testimony showing what type of a person Gene McEnroe

170

was, especially if the colonel decided to find as many character witnesses as Ellen's attorneys had done. But Thompson and Angevine had called a seemingly never-ending list of neighbors and friends to tell how wonderful Ellen's character was, and Geiger clearly didn't want the prosecution to start playing the same game by talking about how fine a fellow Eugene was. He wasn't on trial; Ellen Lunney was.

James McEnroe added that he was hard of hearing sometimes and "do not hear very well for the last couple of years." The jurors may have remembered that he did hear well enough to report that shots were fired across the river near the Lunney farm on two different dates.

∼

Dan McEnroe, the eighteen-year-old brother of Gene, was called by the state.

> On July 24th, I was at Lunney's the fore part of the day. Just went over to be with the boys. I was there in the evening. Patsey and Tom and Willie and I were there. Along about dark a man came with a horse. After he left Willie and I milked three cows and Patsey and Tom went to Dutch Miller's orchard to get some apples. They went about nine. It's about one and a half miles. They were gone about two hours. When they got back we were in the granary.
>
> I remember when they came back. The moon was up. It was a red color and in the southeast. I don't remember whether it was full or not. When they come back we eat the apples they brought, went to the well to get a drink and went back to the granary. Tom and Pat sat in the doorway while I lay in the bed with Willie.
>
> I don't know how many apples they got. I don't know what time we went home. We saw no light in the house. We went to bed in the granary. I slept with Gene – I suppose it was Gene. I noticed somebody was in the bed when I got there. No one else was in the habit of sleeping there. I did not talk with him. No one else talked to him in my hearing. I went to bed a few minutes after going home.
>
> I was awake two or three times during the night. I have sore eyes and they troubled me so that I was restless. I think Gene was in the bed. I woke next morning about daylight. Gene was in the bed.
>
> Gene was there on the 24th of July. I wasn't doing anything at home most of the day. Will Lunney was there and we played croquet. On the

25th, I was at Lunney's a couple of times in the forenoon and in the afternoon I was at Regester's.

I had no particular business at Lunney's. Had a talk with Will and Tom. McKeniff was there the last time I was there.

On the 26th, I was cutting corn for a while in the forenoon and driving the team for Patsey. It was an awful windy day in the afternoon. There was a hot south wind.

Gene went to Dunlap's in the forenoon and to Thuma's. He got home that afternoon. He was not out cutting corn and did not cut any that day. None of us did. It was too windy.

On Friday Patsey and I were cutting corn. Gene came to Norton and did not get back 'till after dark. Pap was with him. They rode in a lumber wagon. On Saturday Pat and I was cutting corn north of the house and west of Lunneys. Gene was around home, around the house. He did not cut any corn after the rape. Patsey and I was cutting corn on Friday. Patsey was not herding any kind of stock on the 27th or 28th.

Patsey had a talk with Nick Dittlinger. He stopped to talk with us.

On cross examination, Dan was asked where Gene was on Sunday and Monday, but the defense objected and the answers he gave were "ruled out," said the *Courier*. Wilder asked where was Eugene on both days, adding, "We are here to prove his whereabouts on those days." Angevine replied that he did not remember ever trying to locate Eugene on those two days. Angevine was proving a stickler of the court rules. At this point in the trial, the state could inquire only about questions raised earlier.

Angevine, cross examining, wanted to know when Dan McEnroe learned of the rape.

"I first learned that Gene was charged with committing rape on Ellen when Patsey told me in the evening," Dan McEnroe testified, saying he did not know about the rape when he twice visited the Lunney household early in the morning.

Patsey told me Gene had been arrested. Gene was not at home on the 25th as I know of. I had been over at Regester's, and when I got back I was told he had been there with the constable. I have talked with Patsey about the case. Have talked it over once or twice with him. It seems to me I talked about where I was that night. I told several – I told some that Gene was home that night when we got home. I talked with father about it.

He asked if Patsey was with me. I did not talk with him about whether

Gene was at home when we got home – well, yes, I guess we did. He asked if Gene was home. I have talked with Patsey about it since Gene was arrested. I have not talked about it recently. It seems as though I did say something about it the other day.

On that same night, Johnnie, Eugene, Patsey and I slept in the granary. There are no windows in the granary – only one door to the west, which was open. I left it open.

The moon rose, I think, at ten forty. I looked at the almanac a couple of days after. Patsey and Tom went for apples at nine o'clock, a distance of one mile and a half. The moon was up before the boys got back. It was not quite rising when we were at the well. I eat four or five apples.

In going home I went south below the stable and then the course is about west, crossed the wire fence – four wires – east of our granary, which is two hundred yards. It was the general path back and forth.

"Johnny? He is about eight or nine years old," Dan McEnroe said, ending his testimony with a brief description of his young brother.

∼

The prosecution had to be concerned about the credibility of the testimony by James and Dan McEnroe. The jury had been told that the sixty-five-year-old father had been cutting fodder for the hogs after sundown while his oldest son lay asleep in bed. And, according to Dan McEnroe, Gene had stopped cutting corn after the rape. Ellen Lunney said seeing Gene in the cornfield across the river from the Lunney home had alarmed her and caused her to fear for her safety. But Dan said Gene was not in the field.

Gene McEnroe's family were providing an alibi for their older brother. They said he went to bed early, about ten o'clock, in the granary. On the days after the rape, they were united in saying that Gene cut no corn fodder during those days. Ellen, clearly, would have been mistaken if she thought Gene was in the corn field. However, the McEnroes were in a pattern of denial about what others said in earlier testimony, and these constant denials could not have helped the state build its case to convict Ellen Lunney of murder.

∼

Patsey McEnroe, the 16-year-old brother of Gene, was called again by the prosecution.

> On Tuesday evening of the 24th of July last, I was at Lunney's. Went before sundown. I saw Dan, Tom and Will there. Dan was not at home when I ate supper. The Lunney boys were up where Gene and me were cutting corn. We were going to bathe and then go for apples.
>
> I saw Tom, Willie, Ellie and Coleman. Dan and Will went to milk the cows and Tom and I went for apples. We were gone nearly two hours. I don't remember if the moon was up when we got back. We eat the apples, got a drink and went home. We were there about an hour.
>
> When we left Lunney's granary there was a light on in our house. It was not lit when we got home. We went to bed in the granary. When we got home Gene was there. Dan slept with Gene. I saw Dan go to bed.
>
> Johnny slept about nine or ten feet north from Gene in the north end of the granary. My bed was a little north and a little east where Dan and Gene slept.
>
> I heard shots that night about an hour after that time. Gene was in bed when I heard the two shots. I had not been asleep. Gene was there the next morning when I woke up. We got up about sunup. I was cutting corn the next day, about 275 yards from Lunneys. I was cutting corn there all day on the 26th. No one helped me.

Did Ellen confuse Gene with his fifteen-year-old brother? He continued,

> I did nothing in the forenoon. In the afternoon I went to Lenora. Dan was helping me. Gene came from town with Muzzy and went to Dunlap's, then to Thuma's and then home to father's. He got there just after dinner.
>
> On the 27th, we hitched a team to cut corn but the team didn't work well and we quit in the afternoon. We tried it with another team, and Dan helped me.
>
> Gene came over to Norton on Friday. He started early in the morning and got home about nine that night. On Saturday he was around the house all day. On the 27th and 28th, I was cutting corn north of the house southwest of Lunneys. Dan and I cut corn all day on the 29th. We were in sight of our own house and Lunney's house most of the time. I was not herding stock on the 27th or 28th.

Patsey was asked about a conversation Nick Dittlinger said he had with the boy. Dittlinger had testified that he talked with Patsey on July 27 or 28 at his stable. Dittlinger said he didn't understand how Gene could have forced Ellen the way he did. Dittlinger quoted Patsey as saying "the damn whore didn't need forcing, that McKeniff had been using her for six months."

"I didn't have a conversation with Dittlinger at any time," said Patsey McEnroe, denying a meeting that Nick Dittlinger said occurred at Dittlinger's stable. "I wasn't at his stable, granary or his house."

Dan, Patsey's older brother, had told the jurors earlier in the day that Patsey "had a talk with Nick Dittlinger," supposedly at Dittlinger's farm.

Didn't he stop at Dittlingers' for a drink of water?

"I didn't go there for a drink of water or any other purpose. I was not on his farm or have any conversation with him at all," replied young Patsey.

Patsey was then cross-examined by Wilder for the prosecution.

"Since the 26th of July last, I have talked about the case with Dan. I don't know how often. It has been talked about considerable since in the family. I talked with father on the 25th. He asked where I was the night before. I don't know if he asked if Gene was with us," Patsey said.

He also denied having a conversation with George Miller, a neighbor.

"I didn't see George Miller the next day," Patsey said. "I did not see or have a conversation with Miller in his corn field after the twenty-fourth of July last. I know where it is. I saw him after but not during that time.

"On the morning of July 25th, I had no talk with my father as to where I had been the night before. I was in the habit of being away in the evening when I desired. Father did not ask me the direct question 'whether or not Gene was with you?'"

George Miller would be the last witness called in the trial. And Miller would report a conversation he had with Patsey.

～

That ended Patsey McEnroe's testimony. Gabriel Dunlap, brother of Anna Dunlap Lunney, was called and testified,

On the 25th of July last, I saw Gene. I remember the fixing of the bond. I went with them to Squire Thuma's. I don't remember seeing him on the 24th. I remember the date of the rape. I believe it was on the 25th we went to Thuma's. He was with Constable Muzzy. We went home to his father's between eleven and twelve – it was after twelve when we got there. I left about half past one after having dinner. It was exceedingly windy. It was a pretty warm wind from the south. I attended a school meeting. I am treasurer of the district and was in a hurry to get around to attend the meeting.

∼

Ellen McEnroe, the eighteen-year-old daughter, was called.

"I am not in good health and have been under the doctor's care since coming to Norton. I am a sister to Gene.

"On the evening of the 24th of July I was at home. I was mending my littler brother's jacket. Father, Gene, Johnny and sister Agnes were at home. Agnes is five and John is nine years old. It was twelve when I wind the clock and started to bed. I undressed sister before I went to bed," she said.

Angevine asked about the mending.

"Before Eugene went to bed I was mending Johnnie's jacket. I begun it at eight and finished it at twelve.

"It was in bad condition," Ellen McEnroe said.

∼

Several witnesses were called to clear up miscellaneous details.

Maggie Siefke, who lived for five years fourteen miles southwest of Lenora, said she was a friend of Ellen Lunney's and had gone to Ellen's county graduating exercises.

"I was there at the home of Ellen the evening before (the rape) and slept with Ellen in the east room upstairs. I was in that room about the time of the killing, I guess. I noticed the ceiling at that time." Maggie Siefke said plaster had been knocked off the ceiling prior to the night she stayed in the room.

She told of an outing, a hayride, at an earlier time when she was with Ellen. "I went home in the wagon with my brother, John McKeniff and Ellen Lunney," she said. "We sat on the bottom of the wagon."

At this point there was an inference by Colonel Jones to the possibility of "hugging and sparking on the tapis," the covering on the bottom of the wagon, between McKeniff and Ellen. The *Norton Champion* said Angevine objected and "the judge and lawyers retired to a council room to discuss the matter, and the audience with the inquisitive reporters were barred from the wisdom in secret displayed."

When the lawyers returned, Jones asked, "How did you ride going back?" Another objection by Angevine brought a sustained objection, and the query went unanswered. However, the colonel knew that the question had been asked, and whether it was answered was not as important as the thought being planted in the jurors' minds that McKeniff and Ellen spent time together on a hayride, "on the bottom of the wagon."

⁓

Clem Sterner, a resident of Almelo township for "eight or seven years," was called. Sterner was a pioneer school teacher who lived in the Almelo community.

"I heard of the alleged crime," Sterner said. "I visited the room in which it is said it occurred. Mr. Lunney took me up. Mrs. Lunney did not go up. She spoke up the stairway. I don't think she was in the room.

"The bed was on the south side of the room. I noticed its ceiling. The bed was a foot from the south side of the room."

⁓

The state rested and the defense offered two witnesses in rebuttal.

James Gilleece said he was at the McEnroe house "the day Gene was buried. I know James McEnroe. I had a conversation with him about the time his sons Patsey and Dan got home the night Ellen was raped. He said they got home between ten and eleven o'clock."

James McEnroe earlier denied he told anyone that Patsey and Dan arrived home between those hours.

⁓

George Miller was called. Miller was the neighbor who helped John Lunney clear his fields when both were early homesteaders.

177

"I know Patsey McEnroe. I saw and talked with him within a day or two after Gene was buried. He said, 'Father came out and asked where we were the night before and I told him.' Then he asked if Gene was with us and, 'I told him no.'"

James McEnroe said he believed Gene had gone to bed early and been asleep in the granary.

~

The defense rested on Wednesday, October 3 at three o'clock. The court adjourned briefly to give the attorneys a chance to read the judges charge to the jury and to make suggestions on the instructions, which would be long.

Fifteen

"G entlemen of the jury," intoned Judge Abel Cutler Tyler Geiger in beginning his instructions to the twelve men on the jury. He started by reading the original information.

It is charged in the information that the defendants, Ellen Lunney, John McKeniff and Thomas Lunney, on the 31st day of July, A. D., 1894, in the county of Norton and the state of Kansas, with the wrongful, malicious, felonious, willful, deliberate and premeditated intent to kill and murder one Eugene McEnroe, then and there being, did then and there, intentionally, wrongfully, unlawfully, maliciously, feloniously, willfully, deliberately, premeditatedly and of their malice and forethought, kill and murder Eugene McEnroe by shooting him, the said McEnroe, with a certain pistol, commonly called a revolver, the said revolver being then and there loaded with powder and leaden balls, and which said pistol, so loaded, the said defendants, Ellen Lunney, John McKeniff and Thomas Lunney, in their hands had held and fired and shot said balls from the said pistol at, against, into and through the body of the said Eugene McEnroe, three mortal wounds, so inflicted as foresaid, the said Eugene McEnroe, in the aforesaid county and state, on the said 31st day of July, A. D., 1984, instantly died.

For reasons unknown to the present-day observer, the information charging the crime gave the original criminal charge to the jury without removing the names of John McKeniff and Tom Lunney. This may have temporarily confused the jury, who had heard the judge dismiss the charges against the two young men. Geiger's next instruction may have added to the confusion as it again listed the three defendants and said that if the guilt is as charged, "the offense so described is known in the law as murder in the first degree."

179

The prosecution showed itself to be inflexible in its determination to prosecute the Lunney case. Why Colonel Jones did not redraft the information is curious, but perhaps he was so busy that he lacked the time. Perhaps he wanted to show everyone around him that he had no secretarial assistance but needed it.

Neither was there any indication that he wanted to reduce the charge against Ellen. The prosecution obstinately pursued the same course it began at the start of the trial, and the fact that the defense may have been winning jurors to its side did not sway the colonel from the goal of convicting Ellen Lunney of first–degree premeditated murder. Did Jones and Wilder talk, or argue, about the wisdom of keeping the original charge instead of reducing it to second-degree murder or manslaughter, or even seeking a plea from Ellen to a lesser charge?

It would not be until the reading of instruction number four, on Geiger's list of forty-nine instructions, that the judge would attempt to clear up the discrepancy of the charge listing McKeniff and Tom Lunney. The colonel could have resolved the problem much earlier if he handled it differently.

> While in the information there are three defendants jointly charged, you are to regard and consider such information as if drawn and charging the defendant, Ellen Lunney alone, the defendants jointly charged with her, Thomas Lunney and John McKeniff, having been heretofore, upon motion, discharged for the reason that the testimony of the state was insufficient to put them upon their defense," said the instruction. "You will heretofore disregard any and all testimony that may have been offered touching the connection of Thomas Lunney and John McKeniff with the crime charged with the defendant Ellen Lunney.

The court file on the Lunney murder case contains several proposed jury instructions offered by the state but rejected by Judge Geiger. Some were "refused as covered by general instructions." Others were rejected outright. The judge and prosecution apparently viewed the law applicable in the Lunney case quite differently, and Geiger's opinion about which case law should be relevant agreed more with what the defense counsel sought than what the prosecutors wanted.

One of the prosecution's proposed but rejected instructions said, "No evil in a person, however extreme, will justify or palliate the taking of his life." The prosecution obviously viewed the idea of excusable homicide in a different light than Geiger or the defense. The "an eye for an eye" type of justice must not have disappeared from life on the Kansas prairie. To accept the prosecution's wording would have barred a defense of justifiable homicide or temporary insanity or any other conceivable defense, and Geiger wasn't about to keep the defense from following that line of thought.

The prosecutors kept trying. Another of Jones' proposed instructions would have said: "The doctrine is that every human being who is in the enjoyment of the right of existence at the particular time and place may be the subject of felonious homicide. Even when the right of life does not exist, this fact is no justification to one extinguishing it otherwise than according to law."

Another proposed page of instructions started in recognizable written English but disintegrated into an unreadable scrawl by the time Colonel Jones came to the bottom of the page. It was as though the bourbon took hold before Jones could finish his cogent thoughts and complete his argument. Jones undoubtedly had been under the stress of a heavy workload.

In contrast, Thompson and Angevine's proposed instructions tended to be treated much better by Geiger. The instructions usually started with a legal citation from Kansas case law, something absent in the prosecution's presentation, typed neatly on the left margin of the paper. Geiger wrote a notation on most of the defense lawyers' submissions that said "adopted" or "allowed."

Two proposed instructions offered by the defense that did not successfully pass Geiger's bench test argued that the information containing the charge was flawed because it lacked specificity and did not charge first- or second-degree murder. The information "does not charge murder in the first degree and you can not find a verdict of murder in the first degree," suggested the defense counsel. Geiger rejected that instruction and a similar one that made the same challenge because it did not specify murder in the second degree.

So the defense didn't receive everything it wanted. Second-degree murder could have proven an alternative to a jury not quite ready to point to Ellen Lunney and say she should be imprisoned for life for first–degree murder. Perhaps that is about where the defense attorneys thought the jury would land in this case.

However, Geiger's instructions turned out to be much more favorable to the defense than the prosecution as he agreed that there should be jury instructions for a "not responsible" verdict in addition to the charges of murder and manslaughter. If Ellen Lunney had been found "not responsible," the result could have been complete freedom. Geiger rewrote most of the defense counsel's proposed instructions, making them more precise. However, the instructions still were long in length out of necessity, the judge told the jury.

> I trust, however, that these instructions about to be read to you are as brief and concise as they reasonably can be to cover the law, which is to aid and give information to you and guide you in the discharge of your duty in arriving at a just, equitable and correct verdict from the evidence submitted herein, and that they will receive at your hands close and careful attention.
>
> The duty resting upon you is a most solemn and serious one. I therefore hope and confidently believe that you will perform it with a full realization of your great responsibility. In deciding questions of fact, you are to be guided by the law and evidence alone, by the evidence which was given during the trial and not from any supposed knowledge of events or occurrences derived from any source other than the testimony given before you in open court; and the law as announced by the court must be your only guide in applying the evidence in this case.
>
> It is your duty as jurors to see that the majesty and purity of the law is upheld and that if the crime charged against the defendants is clearly proven that a proper punishment is meted out. And I further remind you that no man can be lawfully punished, however guilty he may be, until that guilt is first ascertained and declared by a jury of his countrymen.

Judge Geiger's definition of a man obviously included Ellen Lunney. He added,

> On the other hand, the rights of the defendant are sacred to her, and you are in duty bound to be especially careful that no innocent person be pun-

182

ished and disgraced – that no injustice be done her, and that she have the benefit, and be accorded by you, every reasonable doubt as well as that just presumption of innocence and which the law only mercifully, but wisely and justly clothes and invests her.

These were general instructions, ones that Geiger must have used several times in the past before writing them once again in the Lunney case. Geiger soon would get to the heart of the case – a case where many of the instructions turned out to be close to the wording of those suggested by the attorneys for Ellen Lunney.

One could argue that the defense counsel understood Kansas law better than the two prosecutors being paid by the state. Geiger continued:

> You must not allow passion, prejudice or partiality, if any has found a judgment in your mind during the progress of this trial, to influence you in the slightest degree in deciding upon your verdict, but you should and must be guided alone by the law as given you in these instructions, and the evidence of the witnesses as given in your presence.

Jones and Wilder had argued that there should be only one verdict that the jury could reach – murder in the first degree. Geiger told the jurors they could reach several different verdicts on Ellen Lunney: "innocent of the charge made against her," innocent of any degree of crime in any charge made against her, innocent of "each and all of the acts alleged to have been done, or innocent of any material fact necessary to be proven by the state to establish guilt of any offense whatsoever."

The standard for declaring the defendant innocent of a criminal charge was reasonable doubt, Geiger said.

> You are further instructed that you ought not, should not and cannot lawfully convict or acquit the defendant upon any unfair or illogical conclusions drawn from the facts proven, and you have no right to draw any conclusions against the defendant because of any failure on her part to offer any particular kind of proof," said Geiger. "You must try her alone upon the facts proven and not upon conclusions or inferences drawn from facts not proven.

Geiger cautioned that the burden of proof rested upon the state and every ingredient of the charge must be proven beyond a reasonable doubt. If there is a reasonable doubt as to Ellen Lunney's guilt, she must be acquitted. But the standard for deciding that the defendant was guilty of a lesser charge seemed unnecessarily complex. If there were a reasonable doubt of two or more degrees of which she can be found guilty, she can be convicted only of that degree concerning which such reasonable doubt does not exist, the judge said.

Geiger, after his preliminary instructions outlining the charge and general criminal procedures, gave the jury alternatives. They included conviction of first– and second–degree murder but not all the several alternatives of manslaughter that he and the lawyers had discussed.

"Murder is where a person of sound memory and discretion, unlawfully, feloniously kills any reasonable creature in being, and in the peace of the state, with malice aforethought, express or implied," Geiger said. The murder must be done with malice and it must be willful – on purpose.

"If any of the essentials – malice, intent, willfulness, premeditation, deliberation, design, mode of killing or place of killing – is not proven to your satisfaction beyond a reasonable doubt, you should not find the defendant guilty," he said.

Defense counsel must have been happy with such an instruction that said all those essentials had to have been satisfied or Ellen Lunney should be found not guilty.

"Murder in the second degree must have been done purposely and maliciously but without deliberation and premeditation," he said.

"So far as the definition of manslaughter in the first or second degree is concerned, it is omitted from these instructions for the reason that they cannot in any way be deemed applicable to the evidence in this case," Geiger said.

∼

The jury still had plenty of latitude. If it did not want to find Ellen Lunney guilty of first–degree murder because it feared she would be hanged or imprisoned for a long period of time, second-degree murder was available. The difference with murder in the first degree? Murder in the second degree must have been done purposefully and maliciously but without deliberation and premeditation. It would have been difficult to see how Ellen Lunney could have acted without deliberation and premeditation when she took a weapon from a drawer at home, concealed it, walked up behind Eugene McEnroe, pulled the pistol from beneath her cloak and began blasting away with her six-shooter.

Manslaughter in the third or fourth degree also were possible verdicts, Geiger said. Third-degree manslaughter was the killing of another in the heat of passion without a design to defect death. Manslaughter in the fourth degree was defined as the involuntary killing of another, such as in a quarrel. Neither seemed to apply in the Lunney shooting.

~

Then Geiger began a lengthy list of instructions that had been sought by defense counsel. These constituted verdicts that could prove favorable to Ellen Lunney.

First was justifiable homicide. The killing of a person, said the judge, becomes justifiable if it occurs:

1. When resisting any attempt to murder such person or to commit a felony on him or her, or in any dwelling house in which any such person shall be.

2. When committed in the lawful defense of such person, or his or her husband or wife, parent, child, master, mistress, apprentice or servant when there shall be reasonable cause to apprehend a design to commit a felony or do some great personal injury, and there shall be immediate danger of such design being accomplished.

3. When necessarily committed in attempting to apprehend any person for felony.

In addition, homicide is excusable when committed by accident or misfortune in several different ways that did not apply in this case, Geiger explained.

Homicide is excusable when committed by a person in any of the following cases:

A. In lawfully correcting a child, apprentice or servant, or in doing any lawful act with usual or ordinary caution and without any unlawful intent.

B. In the heat of passion upon any sudden or sufficient provocation, or upon any sudden combat, without any undue advantage being taken, and without any dangerous weapon being used, and not done in a cruel and unusual manner.

C. When one, in doing a lawful act, without any intent to hurt, unfortunately chances to kill another.

"And if under any of these definitions of justifiable or excusable homicide, any killing that may have been proven to have been committed by the defendant was excusable or justifiable under the circumstances proven in this case, then the defendant is neither guilty of murder or manslaughter in any degree," read the instruction completing the jury's charge on justifiable and excusable homicide.

Geiger's view of the law on justifiable homicide gave the jurors something they could grab onto if they found that Ellen Lunney was acting in self defense. Did the instructions on justifiable or excusable homicide fit the situation in the Lunney case? Probably not, but that would be for the jury to decide. Geiger did not place a time restriction in the jury instructions on the period in which a wrong could fester and stimulate passion, leaving it to the lawyers to argue whether a week was too long a time to have lapsed between a rape and a killing in response to it.

~

The judge quoted verbatim several instructions on insanity offered by the defense counsel, and these provided the jury with enough room to free Ellen Lunney from the charge of first–degree murder. If the jurors wanted to find Ellen Lunney entered a period of madness, they could sift through these instructions:

"If you believe from the evidence that at the time the defendant, Ellen Lunney, shot and killed Eugene McEnroe was insane, you must find her not guilty and it is immaterial whether the insanity was permanent or momentary," said one instruction helpful to a defense attorney in closing arguments.

"If at the moment the shots were fired, she, the defendant, was insane, she is not guilty of any degree of homicide, and you must find her not guilty," said another instruction.

"There are many different causes which produce insanity and it assumes many different forms. A person may be sane at one time and insane at another. She may be insane on one subject and perfectly sane on another. Such a person can be held criminally responsible only for acts done on a subject on which, and at a time, she is sane," said a third instruction.

It does not devolve upon the defendant to prove that she was insane at the time of the criminal acts. The jurors are the sole judges of Ellen Lunney's state of mind and the "provocation" upon her. If the jury had reasonable doubt as to whether the provocation was sufficient or not, "you should find her not guilty," said the judge.

It was not a question of whether Ellen Lunney knew the difference between right or wrong generally. The question was whether "she knew the difference between right and wrong in regard to the very act with which she is charged. If some controlling emotion or feeling was in truth the acting power within her which she could not resist, or if she had not sufficient use of her reason to control the passion or emotion which prompted her, she under the law would not be responsible," Geiger told the jury.

One could draw the conclusion that Judge Geiger steered the jury toward a verdict of temporary madness.

The jury might have found the instructions lengthy and burdensome. But it appears that Geiger had tried hard to be fair. He had agreed with the defense counsel that instructions should have given the jurors the options of finding justifiable or excusable homicide or for insanity or temporary insanity. These defense counsel instructions were printed almost verbatim from suggested language Clint Angevine and Lafe Thompson gave Geiger that included citations from Kansas cases. It appears, on the matter of jury instructions at least, that the defense attorneys were far better prepared in providing relevant jury instructions. Thompson and Angevine got much of what they wanted the jury to hear from Geiger's lips.

Would those rules be enough for the jury to issue a not guilty verdict? Or would the jury remember the coolness with which the defendant walked up behind Eugene McEnroe and gunned him down and decide that was sufficient to be murder in the first degree? After all, that seemed to be the view that Ellen's neighbors in Lenora believed.

Sixteen

The time arrived for counsels' closing arguments. Closings, in the 1890s, could be lengthy as the attorneys wove their cases together to describe how events had transpired. In this case, closing came after the judge's instructions to the jury.

First it was the prosecution's turn. At different times Colonel Jones and Ledru Wilder would address the jury, with Jones taking the lead in the case. This division of labor probably was a strategy devised for focusing the skills of both attorneys in describing their case to the jury. It could also have been because of the weariness of the prosecutors after a lengthy trial. Both attorneys believed strongly in their case and argued forcibly for a murder conviction.

Jones began by saying there was no doubt who committed the murder of Eugene McEnroe. But Jones would not give up on what had been his original strategy. He refused to admit that Ellen Lunney had been raped. Or, if she had been raped, he argued that it was by John McKeniff, not Eugene McEnroe and immaterial to the murder.

Jones talked about "the willfulness, deliberation and maliciousness of the defendant in the execution of her crime."

He described the actions of Tom Lunney and John McKeniff in the Thuma School on the day of the homicide and his theory that the killing was contemplated and planned by the family, "and that they wished to locate Eugene McEnroe so that Ellen could go and shoot him."

Jones said Ellen Lunney was shown to be "cool, strong and determined, so strong that Bob Regester could not take the revolver from her and had to rely on George Miller to assist him, so cool and determined that she approached her victim undaunted."

In reviewing the "means of escape," the prosecutor said that "the means were not good but the best they had. They could not be expected to procure conveyances better than they had, a light buggy and a light team. Just as soon as the shots were fired, Tom Lunney was at hand to take Patsey McEnroe away, and McKeniff was at her side to take Ellen to the buggy.

"What did she put the revolver in her pocket for? She was in no danger of being disturbed by Eugene McEnroe that day. Her protection was assured," Jones argued, beginning his attack on several aspects of Ellen Lunney's testimony.

"It is claimed that after the rape the aggravation to her caused by the circulation of stories about her character invented, or claimed by the defense to be invented, by the McEnroes caused her stress and anguish. But the claims that Patsey McEnroe told the 'damned whore' story to Nick Dittlinger while Patsey was herding cattle near him falls to the ground. He was proven to be cutting corn that day, at no time herding cattle, and while a conversation may have taken place near the cornfield with Dittlinger, it is denied by two present that such a conversation as testified to ever took place.

"Again, she claims to have seen Eugene McEnroe parading in her view in a cornfield, which worried her considerably, too, but it is clearly proven that he was then away securing bonds and did not return until noon. Hence, these two props to her story about her aggravation must fall to the ground."

Focusing on the Lunney home and the scene of the rape, Jones argued that Ellen's retiring in her drawers and her chemise – the night clothes in which she was raped – was most unlikely. Wouldn't she have changed to something else? And slept in a different bed?

The attorney also dwelled at some length on the moon and its location.

"The preponderance of evidence goes to show that the light was not so good as the girl claims. From the evidence it would appear that the moon was in the southeast and could not have shown on the bed in the southwest corner of a room, shining through one east window," the Colonel said.

He contended that there was no visible means of a struggle in the bed. The bed was not broken down in the struggle to "maintain her virtue." When Eugene McEnroe's hand was over her mouth, "she could have bitten it. She could have marked, scratched or maimed Eugene McEnroe with her loose arms.

"She comes before us as a virgin, as a woman who had never known man. When she was there asleep before the entrance, he must have done a great deal of fumbling, he must have handled her and under the laws of experience and metaphysics his touch ought to have startled her because it was unfamiliar and unusual," he said.

The prosecutor took the drawers before the jury and argued the impossibility of intercourse.

"Is it reasonable that they would have you believe that a girl so sensitive, so shattered in spirits could have been driven insane? Could it be that she continued sleeping after such an alleged crime upon her person in the very bed immediately after?

"It is one of those impossible things. They must come to us with another and better story."

The colonel placed the responsibility for proving the rape upon the defendant.

"In this case the undisputed evidence shows that after the alleged rape no medical examination of the private parts of the defendant ever occurred," Jones said. "It is the duty of the defendant, at once, after the alleged rape occurred, to have a medical examination, and the failure to do so brings discredit of the evidence that such an act happened."

The *Champion* noted impressively that Jones led into his arguments with great force.

"Colonel Jones, during the first twenty minutes of his speech, easily surpassed himself and surprised his audience. With the free flow of oratory and argumentative artifice let forth from the flood gates of his sympathetic bosom. But as he proceeded he grew weaker and weaker to the diminishing point. He looked fatigued and worried over the case which must excuse the anti-climax in the address to the jury. Almost two weeks of incessant labors on the case told on his constitution. He spoke almost two hours in closing the argument for the state."

The character of the defendant, her brother Tom and John McKeniff became central to the state's arguments. The defense attorneys obviously had anticipated the attack with its long list of character witnesses for Ellen Lunney.

The prosecutors tore directly at the character of Ellen Lunney, which had been defended by a lengthy list of neighbors, former classmates and families with whom she lived in Norton. Tom Lunney and John McKeniff were portrayed as scouts who located Eugene McEnroe in Thuma School so Ellen could kill him.

"The two young men arranged the escape and the route for the young woman. Ellen sat in the buggy awaiting her fate, whatever it was to be, but it never appeared she tried to flee," Jones said.

The *Norton Champion*, in a column of local news items next to the reporting of the story of the court trial, criticized the colonel for his handling of Anna Lunney. The item was in the October eleven paper, the same one that listed the jury instructions.

"The abuse heaped upon the head of old lady Lunney by the county attorney was scandalous, vicious and reprehensible. Mrs. Lunney was not on trial. It is high time that courts put a stop to these vicious attacks of attorneys upon witnesses and innocent persons. These attacks under the protection of courts are becoming very tiresome to a people who believe in fair play and justice, and there should be an emphatic demand for reform in this manner."

Hull, of the populist Liberator newspaper, also criticized prosecutor Jones in a news column.

"In our report of the murder of Eugene McEnroe, we stated the rumor that there had been illicit relations between her and John McKeniff, which it had been designed to cover up. We are very sorry we so stated. We were misled by our overzealous county attorney. We believe that nothing could be farther from Miss Lunney's true character. She is very far from being an amative woman.

Indeed a man of strong passions would disgust her. That she was a virgin before the rape she unconsciously demonstrated when she stated she was "awakened by a sharp pain." This is not generally known even among women, all of whom have experienced it, and she could only have known of it by experiencing it. Let us further say that we believe Ellen Lunney is no more responsible for shooting Eugene McEnroe than our pencil was for perpetrating the scandal connecting her and McKeniff."

~

The state – anticipating the defense's argument about insanity or temporary madness – disputed the idea that Ellen Lunney had an "uncontrollable impulse" that led to killing Eugene McEnroe.

"It is possible that an uncontrollable impulse is sometimes sufficient to destroy criminal responsibility, but this probably only so when it destroys the power of the accused to comprehend rationally the nature, character and consequences of the particular act, and not when the accused still has the power of knowing the character of the particular acts and that they are wrong," Ledru Wilder argued, taking up where an exhausted Colonel Jones ended his summation. "The law will not recognize the theory that any uncontrollable impulse may so take possession of a person's faculties and powers as to compel her to do what she knows to be wrong, and a crime, and relieve her of any criminal responsibility."

Wilder knew the defense would be talking about "criminal responsibility" and wanted to defuse the issue with the jurors. Prosecutors everywhere have argued that a woman who takes a gun to shoot a man is a criminal and not crazy. And defense attorneys everywhere know that jurors often are reluctant to say a woman is justified in killing the man and might decide that she was not responsible because of a temporary state of mind.

"When a person at the time of the crime has sufficient mental capacity to understand the nature and quality of the crime, and the mental capacity to know whether they are right or wrong, she is responsible for the act," Wilder argued. "If she does not possess this degree of capacity, she is not responsible."

"When a passion or uncontrollable offense is set up as a defense to a crime, the role that the jury must keep before their eyes and minds in determining the responsibility of the defendants is this: Was the accused at the time of doing the act complained of conscious of the nature of her act, or did she know that it was felonious homicide?

"The inherent and universal rule of the law is that killing, to be justifiable, must be done in prevention of a felony and not for the punishment thereof in satisfaction of personal revenge or wounded feelings," Wilder said, adding some information for the jury that Judge Geiger had refused to place in his formal instructions.

"Hence, the right of self defense of chastity, even to the taking of a life, results from the resistance to the commission of an act. This right proceeds alone from necessity," Wilder said.

"And however complete it may be, or however far the law permits it to be carried, it stops where necessity ends."

The prosecution concentrated on the fact that the killing of Eugene McEnroe occurred a week after the alleged rape, which Wilder said virtually negated the self defense argument used by Thompson and Angevine.

"Mere excitement will not reduce killing to manslaughter," said Wilder, who also spoke for two hours. The prosecution clearly had set its sights on murder in the first degree and wanted the jury to understand that the state's goal was not a conviction for a lesser crime.

Seventeen

Lafayette Thompson then took his turn in presenting the defense's closing argument. Thompson said the defense did not contend there was no killing, just that Ellen Lunney was not guilty of homicide. He gave two excuses for her act – justifiable or excusable homicide and unaccountability – "either of which clears her of guilt."

Thompson avoided using the terms "insanity" or "temporary insanity," preferring "unaccountability." Juries were unpredictable when faced with deciding whether a person was "insane." Even if the jury could see some evidence of insanity, the question of how much a defendant should be held responsible, and what kind of punishment should be meted out, has vexed juries and judges for years. Juries tended to use their own common sense in deciding such issues, ignoring the precise language of the law.

Prosecutor Wilder had challenged the defense to show any external signs of a struggle during the alleged rape. In response, Thompson referred to a "lameness" by Ellen and scrape wounds on both her knees. He said the "fiend was on her in her moment of innocence and sleep, hand over her mouth. She fought like a lioness for her cubs, for that priceless jewel of womanhood, her chastity."

Her chastity, he said, was something she was prepared to die for.

Thompson attacked the McEnroes' attempts to provide Eugene with an alibi.

"If I ever had a doubt about the rape and Eugene McEnroe as the guilty party, those alibis would dispel it," he said, beginning an attack on testimony by several members of the McEnroe family.

Thompson said he excluded the father, James McEnroe, for the part he took in trying to clear his son's name of the crime. He said that the old gentleman, "in his dreams only," went out to cut corn at midnight to feed the pigs.

"What for? To have it to say to the two lads away junketing around the country stealing apples, 'Ain't you ashamed of yourselves to let your poor old rheumatic father cut corn for the hogs at twelve o'clock at night?' No, but to tell this jury the untruth that Eugene was then in bed in the granary at that time.

"And what is the scheme that they have to establish that hour? Why, the daughter Ellen was up to that time patching a jacket – patching a jacket for the little boy from eight o'clock that night to twelve o'clock. It must have gone through a threshing machine."

He ridiculed the idea of Patsey lying there in bed for an hour and a half watching Eugene for fear he would go and rape Ellen Lunney – "lying there, after rambling over the country stealing apples and over an hour watching the innocent Eugene."

"Everything they do fastens the guilt more strongly on Eugene. What other motive had the defendant for killing Eugene McEnroe? Why should she kill him if he did not commit the rape? What have they to show a purpose? Absolutely nothing, not even the flimsiest theory. The only ones the state could say committed that rape was Coleman, who appeared before you on this stand, or McKeniff, who was miles away that night."

Thompson spoke of the theory that Eugene could not have known that Ellen was alone that night. He theorized that Patsey and Dan told Eugene about her isolation in the house on their return and that they were always cognizant that the rape was committed by their brother. Thompson said he deplored the management of a family that would send Eugene to bed to enjoy sweet sleep so he could get up early, yet permit a poor girl, now under the doctor's care, to sit up to twelve o'clock mending a garment.

"The girl was the first to get up in the morning to get breakfast," Thompson said. "There was no fairness in such a treatment."

Thompson talked about the insanity plea, saying it frequently was feigned and put on for a purpose. To account for the temporary and sudden aberration of Ellen's mind, he followed her from the proud moment of her life, her graduation from high school and the obtaining of a teaching certificate, through the scenes of her rape and the misery and sorrow, up to the minute when the shots were fired – "scenes, thoughts, hopes, despairs and agonies enough to drive the sanest person mad, crazy, deranged," he said.

"Her extreme power at that moment proved her frenzied beyond her nature, insanely strong beyond her normal strength," he said.

Thompson then referred briefly to a local case described by the *Champion* as a sudden insanity of a person in the city of Norton as an example of how quick a change in the mind can occur.

The newspaper said the defense attorney reached the climax of his oratorical effort as he described "the virgin sleeper on her couch of innocence and the velvet-footed demon tiptoeing on his amorous pilgrimage to the girl, the coy and hot-breath passion held in check for the pounce, the pain and the awakening – the recognition by the moonbeams shining upon him in full, a light placed by the heavenly God to expose to view the villain who destroyed her forever."

He described her paleness and her weird look soon after entering the door of the schoolhouse. Thompson depicted that look as "insanity" and the fact that she rapidly pulled the trigger of the revolver, firing five shots. He asserted,

"But if there had been twenty-five, all would have been fired under the impulse, every shot fatal, every shot hitting Eugene McEnroe, when she could not in her normal state hit a tree in an equal number of trials, which goes to confirm the fact that she was at the instant out of her reason, insane, unaccountable for the homicide."

As to the provocation for the killing, Thompson drew a picture of two varied careers of lovers once engaged but later gone astray, the seducer and the seduced, the raper and the raped.

"The former goes through the world achieving honors, political preferment and fame, sermons of eulogy, floral tributes with bands playing the dead march in Saul, newspaper columns inverted and praise without stint.

"The latter receives a note in an obscure corner of the journals reading: 'Old Moll was found dead last night in an outhouse of Blank's gambling den and will be buried in Potter's field.'

"The woman has no protection, no safety under the law and the course pursued by Ellen Lunney is the one that should receive the endorsement of humanity.

"It was a matter of her chastity."

Thompson had hit upon what had become the central issue of the trial. Judge Geiger's definition of justifiable homicide did not quite fit the situation, and juries traditionally have not liked to decide whether someone is suffering from madness, even if it is temporary. Anger at the loss of her chastity would become another defense that the jury could use to acquit Ellen.

Ellen Lunney had no protection, nor did women everywhere in America in the 1890s, from rapists like Eugene McEnroe. They could not plead self defense to cover the anger of revenge at being the victims of vicious attacks if a period of time had elapsed between the act and the retaliation. The prosecutors in Norton County argued the law at the time in the case of Ellen Lunney, not an abstract idea of what they believed. Women did not possess the legal ability to respond to a rape except as Ellen did a week after the event. She did what she felt was necessary to protect herself and her chastity. When she lost her chastity, she had no recourse but to kill her defiler, the tarnisher of her virginity and her honor. The defense spent considerable time talking about the purity of women.

"When your duty is done here, and you go to your homes, go in that consciousness of duty well performed. And when you meet that loved companion through all the trials and vicissitudes of life, you can imprint upon her virtuous lips the kiss of an honest husband and say to her: 'My dear wife, I have given my verdict as the light of reason shone and as justice dictated, and I gave it in favor of protection to woman's honor and the sanctity of the home.'

"When the little one, the baby girl, meets you at the gate, claps her chubby hands in glee at the return of her father and entwines her loving arms around your neck and imprints the kiss of the childish soul upon your brow, you can hold her in your fatherly embrace and say, 'My darling girl, before my God and my neighbors, I have rendered my verdict for the purity of girlhood, of womanhood, and in favor of virtue, home and happiness.'"

And so saying, Thompson concluded two hours of his part of the defense arguments.

$\sim$

The jury recessed for dinner, the noon meal. The jurors would return for more defense appeals for their client, this time from Clinton Angevine.

Thompson had managed to warm the courtroom with his talk of chastity, purity and virginity and his praise of motherhood, woman's honor, home and happiness. When Angevine began speaking at one–thirty in the afternoon, the courtroom again was filled, said the *Champion*, "beyond standing room, every seat and aisle being occupied with a close listener, a clever number of whom were women."

While the jury consisted of twelve males, the women would dominate the audience. They came to support Ellen Lunney, to watch how the system of justice would deal with rape and revenge. The *Champion* indicated that the women came as partisan advocates for the defendant.

Angevine cleared his throat. "The first definition in the instructions is that where a person of such sound discretion and memory unlawfully and feloniously kills another, he is guilty of murder in the first degree," he said, placing emphasis on the words "sound discretion and memory."

Angevine recounted the acts of Ellen Lunney up to the time of the shooting. He asked the jury to say beyond a doubt that she was responsible for the conditions or culpable for the act. The defense lawyer concluded that the jury could not do so and she was not guilty of murder in the first degree.

He discussed the instruction that said homicide is the killing of a person in "the heat of passion," or "upon a sudden and sufficient provocation," and such killing is excusable.

"Eugene McEnroe's crime was heinous and the atonement that

was made was terrible, but under the law will you answer, what was the provocation? She was infamously treated by Eugene McEnroe in the rape. He lied about her, slandered her, laughed at her, leered – how far would this conduct have to go to be sufficient to provoke a sudden homicide?" asked Angevine.

He reviewed briefly the complications in the argument of prosecutor Wilder, "who contended half the time that there was no rape committed" on Ellen Lunney and then tried to prove that "Ellen Lunney committed that deed through malice and revenge, and that she killed Eugene McEnroe through malicious revenge."

"How absurd! Wilder would have that girl while she was being raped – everybody knows that a woman when being raped is so scared, so alarmed, unable to use her strength through fear – I say Wilder would have her gouge out an eye or bite off an ear and take it into court as an identification of the rapist. You read of rape cases every day, and where did you ever hear of any woman ever taking into court a piece of the man to prove who did the crime?"

He viewed the case under the prosecution's theory that no rape was committed and demanded:

"What was the motive in killing Eugene McEnroe if he were innocent? Upon what scheme, what excuse, what theory will the overzealous state explain the killing of an innocent man by this girl, this timid, reserved, modest, virtuous girl? Can any reasonable motive be assigned? If she invented such a story it would prove her insane. No motive was offered, none could be offered, none whatever!"

Like Thompson, Angevine attacked the actions of the McEnroe family for "fabricating an alibi."

"They began fabricating an alibi as soon as they learned Ellen's story. But it is very dangerous to prove an alibi by three or four persons. Unless they have their story well learned, one of them will give the snap away. How well was the fabrication contrived? Let us see.

"After the old man McEnroe stayed up to twelve o'clock to feed the pigs, Ellen McEnroe to patch from eight to twelve and a little girl nine years old asleep with her clothes on forced by the plot to open one eye to inquire the time, all three to prove it was midnight before the boys returned to find Eugene asleep in the granary some time after that hour.

"Let us go back. On the day Gene was arrested, Mr. Miller testified that old man McEnroe called one of the boys to him and inquired, 'Where was Gene last night? Was he over to the Lunneys with you?' What did he tell Gilleece and Donohoe on the day of the funeral? A story contradictory in every aspect – a story strangely in variance with the one he gives on the stand. In the one he saw the four boys in their innocent beds during the time of the rape. In the other, only two were there and two were away returning at an hour unknown to him. What faith can you have in such an alibi? Has it not every earmark and trace of a manufactured alibi? Its bungling manufacture only goes to show that they knew Eugene was the culprit and had committed the rape.

"If the whole family knew that Eugene was asleep in the granary, why circulate such scandalous stories about her character? Why did his brother say 'Eugene did not have to force her. The damn whore has been running with John McKeniff for the last six months?' Why circulate such abominations of this pure girl unless to break down her credibility and defeat her in the court? Does it not clearly prove that the alibi, which would have cleared him, was manufactured after the shooting? What people are they who resort to such infamy? As the poet says,

> *They are neither man nor woman,*
> *They are neither ghost nor human,*
> *They are ghouls.*

"Before that night her home life was a song of joy, since then a paradise lost. What she was before that crime, she will never be again."

Angevine went over the testimony of Patsey McEnroe and concluded that "Patsey is in the impeaching business with a big job on his hands – impeaching Nick Dittlinger to whom he unquestionably told the story of Ellen's loose character."

Angevine urged the jury against compromising with a conviction of manslaughter.

"We are not asking for any compromise in this case. What is a verdict to Ellen Lunney? So far as she is concerned she may spend the balance of her days in the penitentiary or anywhere else so far as her earthly happiness is concerned.

"Manslaughter is a stamp of untruth upon her story. A conviction is a warrant to every rapist. Go and despoil every virgin you can approach. Invent what story you please. The law will clear you. The courts will hear you out. Rather, give the world the authority to repeat that the home may be protected, chastity may be secured, womanhood defended, and truth and honor vindicated."

Angevine thus concluded his arguments, which lasted two and a half hours.

~

It was nearly four-thirty in the afternoon before Colonel C. D. Jones had his chance for his final closing, his last chance to persuade the jury that the defendant Ellen Lunney should be found guilty of murder in the first degree. He told the jurors they should uphold the law.

"The state is here simply asking of you to perform your duty. It is our province to defend the statutes of the state in the punishment of crime," Jones said.

The *Norton Champion* said the Colonel made an impassioned appeal to the jury, saying he was the father of two girls reaching womanhood and whose existence is entangled in every fiber of his heart. But Jones said he did not wish the jury to give precedent to the act of any woman that would take from him his heart–cherished son.

He still focused on the location of the moon.

"To go no farther than the testimony of her own witness, it is absolutely established that the moon rose on that night in the southeast, and that instead of shining upon the bed in the southwest corner of the room, as a matter of fact it shone through the window, shone over in the northwest corner of that room, making darker that corner of the room where the bed is alleged to have been."

Jones held up the drawers before the jury. He argued,

"These were worn by her that night, buttoned, unopened as you see, and we are asked to believe that Eugene McEnroe committed a rape upon the wearer who never before knew any man. It is the flimsiest nonsense ever presented to any reasonable set of beings. Sift this testimony. Reason upon it as you would in your everyday business, and you can never conclude that such a rape was thus committed."

Earlier, the prosecution had argued that if a rape occurred, it was done by Coleman, the evening visitor who offered a stallion for breeding, or by the Irishman McKeniff. Jones then shifted to defending the McEnroes.

"It is unfair to charge the McEnroes with fabrication in the explanations made as to why and how they were up so long of the night of July 24. Their alibi manufactured would not bring back to them their dead brother, the dead son in his tomb. They have not the interest in this case as have the Lunneys. Where is their gain in this much scoffed fabrication?"

Jones again discussed the testimony that Ellen Lunney retired to the very room in which the alleged rape occurred, going to bed in the very bed upon which she had been a few moments before, falling asleep among the falling plaster and sleeping so soundly that in the morning the brothers pass through that room and go downstairs without waking her.

"Is it reasonable that they would have you believe her to be so sensitive, so sheltered in spirits as to be driven insane? Could it be done, sleeping after such an alleged crime upon her person, sleeping in the very bed immediately after? It is one of those impossible things, and they must come to us with another and better story," Jones said.

∼

The *Champion* commented on the closing arguments. "It may be said as a general summary of the critical place assigned to the four addresses that Wilder's was the most adroit, Thompson's the most touching and sympathetic, Angevine's the most convincing and argumentative and Jones' the most eloquent," said the newspaper.

Those who thought the jury's deliberation might be brief were wrong. The deliberations lasted seventeen hours, leading some to speculate that it would be a hung jury. But on Friday, October 5, at five o'clock in the afternoon the jury sent word to the judge and attorneys that it had reached a verdict.

The word that the jury was returning spread quickly though the town, and fifteen minutes later the courtroom filled with towns-people to hear the jury's verdict.

Lafe Thompson sat down in the defense counsel's chair, gave an inquiring glance at the jury and placed his head upon the palm of his hand – ready for the "worst verdict that could befall his client," said the *Champion*.

"The prisoner was brought in but her usual paleness was not more remarkable, nor her utter impassiveness any the more dis-turbed or excited. She only once looked over towards the jury, sit-ting as ever with her eyes on the floor, head tipped to the left shoulder, lips compressed and seemingly turned to marble," the ever alert J. W. Conway of the *Champion* noted.

Judge Geiger inquired whether a verdict had been reached? It had, said the foreman, S. A. Winklepleck, who handed the verdict to the clerk. Judge Geiger asked the clerk, Dan Hart, to read the verdict.

"NOT GUILTY," read the clerk.

The *Champion* reported that the courtroom erupted in bedlam. Cheers rang from the crowd, which had become heavily partisan in favor of the young defendant. Spectators tossed their hats into the air. Hands clapped. The crowd rejoiced with yells. Tears appeared in the eyes of many, especially the Lunney family, but also those of Lafe Thompson and Clint Angevine – both of whom had become deeply involved emotionally in the rape-murder case.

"The defendant wept almost as hard as Lafe Thompson," said the *Champion*.

"The courtroom was the scene of more sympathetic joy than will ever again in our time be experienced," concluded the *Champion*.

Epilogue

Time never stands still, and the events of the summer and autumn of 1894 left their mark on many of the people involved. Other, unrelated events brought more permanent change to the towns and farms of the High Plains.

For years, until the midtwentieth century, many of the strongest western Kansas towns continued to grow. Then some of the smaller towns began diminishing significantly in size, becoming swallowed up by the prairie that had helped sustain them and their economies, which usually were one dimensional, dependent almost entirely on the agriculture from their hinterland. By the year 2000, those lacking economic viability had fallen into decline, and many of the towns-people and the outlying country folk had moved elsewhere.

Lenora remained home to a grade and high school that educated the children from the surrounding area until the community began a gradual disintegration similar to what was happening to many of the plain's towns of the same size. At midtwentieth century in Lenora, three and sometimes four groceries and several restaurants served the needs of its residents and those living nearby. Businesses prospered, and an empty storefront along the main streets seldom remained vacant for long. A doctor and dentist served local needs. The economy remained healthy even though some of the usual customers of the town's businesses began driving to Norton, Oberlin or Hill City or other larger towns to buy at the supermarkets and stores that offered more choices and lower prices. The decline sapped the town's energy. By 2005, Lenora lacked the basic services and a high school that are common to economically viable towns of the area. The high school closed in 2001 because of a shortage of students.

New Almelo, which never incorporated, saw a similar decline by the end of the twentieth century, although even in its best years it never amounted to more than two score scattered buildings. By 2000 the Catholic Church, without a pastor except for a circuit-riding priest or deacon who came by on special occasions, stopped services and mass on most Sundays.

～

Political change came more gradually, except in the case of the populists. The People's Party, which had done so well in the Kansas elections of 1892, suffered a serious defeat two years later but rebounded briefly in 1896.

The prosecutors continued prosecuting. Ledru Wilder was elected county attorney in 1896, and again in 1906 and 1914. Colonel C. D. Jones was elected to his old job again in 1898. Lafe Thompson would win a seat on the District Court bench for two years and in 1904 served again as county attorney. Most of Thompson's years were spent in private practice. He was described in 1912 as "one of the leading men of the legal fraternity." A. C. T. Geiger remained on the bench for another decade then returned to private practice, listing several large corporations among his clients. Clint Angevine participated in a case in Jewell County in 1898 but seemed to practice mainly in Kansas City, Kansas. His firm is recorded as Angevine & Cubbison, located in the Portsmouth Building in Kansas City. He and his wife Nettie had at least two daughters, Georgia and Marie. Angevine was alive in 1925 but had died by 1928. The 1929 Kansas City, Kansas, City Directory lists Nettie as being the widow of Clinton Angevine.

Most of the McEnroes moved away. James, the father, died in January 1896, less than two years after the trial. Since he died intestate, an administrator was appointed to handle his will. His survivors were listed in documents filed in Norton County District Court. One was Catherine Dunlap, who had married Gabe Dunlap and who was a cousin of Ellen and the rest of the Lunney family. Gabe, Anna Lunney's brother, had provided bond for Eugene after the latter was charged with Ellen Lunney's rape.

The McEnroes did not survive the depression in Norton County. Not long after James McEnroe's death, Pamelia Weston filed a civil lawsuit in District Court in Norton asking for foreclosure on the McEnroe farm. Weston said that James McEnroe obtained a $500 mortgage from the Security Investment Company in March 1889 that was payable March 1, 1894. Then the mortgage was extended to March 1897 and transferred to Pamelia Weston. Because the interest on the loan had not been paid, the plaintiff sought the full amount, $560, plus costs, for a total of $598. The McEnroes could not find $598 to meet the mortgage payment and lost their entire farm.

Some of the McEnroe family moved to eastern Kansas.

Patsey McEnroe, like his older brother Eugene, had an abbreviated life. In 1899 he went to Leavenworth, Kansas, and enlisted in the U. S. Army's 44th Infantry. He was sent to the Philippines. After about two years he was mustered out of the Army so he could serve in the Metropolitan Police force in Manila. He resigned from that job and entered the livery business in Manila, but he gave up that work when some local residents burned his barn. Patsey became a teamster for a time and prepared to return to Kansas when he was stricken with cholera. Patsey died in August 1902, according to a letter received by his sister Agnes, who then lived in St. Paul, Kansas. He was buried in a military cemetery in Lucena, the Philippines.

Dan McEnroe seemed to have disappeared from Norton County.

∾

The Lunney family's ordeal from the rape, murder and trial had ended, and they took their daughter Ellen home with them on October 5. It was the first time she had been out of the custodial care of Sheriff Betterton since July 31, when she had been arrested.

The family would have had a weekend of quiet celebration as relatives and friends came to the Lunney farm to pay their respects and wish Ellen well.

But it would be a long time before the Lunney murder case

would stop being a topic of conversation in the nearby towns of Lenora and New Almelo. The rape, murder and trial would have long-term effects on the major actors and actresses in the drama that was played out in a courtroom twenty-five miles away. The Lunneys decided that it was best to forget about the tragedy of 1894, hoping that the community eventually would forget, too.

The *Norton Champion* had a few words of fascinating speculation about what may have happened in the case, some information that neither the *Champion* nor the *Courier* had mentioned during the trial and the editor's opinions about whether the jury reached the correct verdict. In the following, it's uncertain what came from court testimony or what editor Conway imagined, but his story is included. He wanted to share it with his readers before the subject dropped off the front pages of the local newspapers, and although it is confusing, Conway's words will be shared here:

> There are three opinions about equally divided on this case:
>
> 1 – There was no rape. There is something back of the apparent conduct, and Ellen Lunney is, therefore, a cold-blooded murderer.
>
> 2 – The rape was committed by Eugene McEnroe, but he ought to have been punished by imprisonment. Death was greater than his crime, and she should be punished to equalize the two offenses.
>
> 3 – The rape was committed, death was deservedly dealt to the rapist then or later, and Ellen Lunney was the proper Nemesis.
>
> How the first opinion can find judgment in a reasonable brain we are at a loss to know. It is one of those unaccountable impressions that find lodgement in a manner not to be traced from anything to be recited in the history of the case, from any developments of testimony, nor from the probable impetus of human conduct.
>
> It cannot be reconciled to the moving motive of the tragic act, nor adjustable to the conditions intimating a homicide.
>
> We argued at some length after the affair occurred and before the trial that the most depraved, groveling and heartless woman on earth could not kill her friend, companion, neighbor to cover up any indiscretion of her own, knowing that the victim is innocent. Much less, then, could such a thing be done by one whose character is the boast and pride of her acquaintances and companions.
>
> Eugene McEnroe, because his character good or bad was not placed in

evidence, ought not to be assailed now. There seems to be an explanation of his conduct at hand: Why did he, a confessedly good boy, commit the rape, and why did he linger around after doing so?

There are two questions that ought to bring out answers hinting his innocence.

It seems plain to us that when his two brothers arrived at the granary on the night of July 24 some such conversation as this would in all reason occur:

"What kept you over to Lunneys so long."

"O we were after apples and waiting for Lunneys to return."

"Where were they?"

"Visiting 15 miles away – all but Ellen, Tom and Will."

Sleep followed to all but Eugene.

No telling what thoughts then came over him, love or passion: But in our opinion he never left that bed with the remotest idea of committing a rape.

Arriving at the age of twenty-six, it appears that his gallantries with the women were an unknown quantity and it seems that his methods of love-making were not smoothed by varied experience.

He was just in the condition of life, through ignorance of the other sex and inexperience, to undertake the accomplishment of his desires through force rather than persuasion; although we think that he never left his own bed with forcible designs on the person of Ellen Lunney.

What does he discover on entering her room? A sleeping beauty, adorned in gown and draped by moonlight. Irresistible: a sight to make the heart throb in lawless passions.

He touched her, perhaps whispered.

She did not move.

He leaned over her, embraced her.

She did not awake.

Perhaps he flattered himself with the delusion that she feigned sleep and then he proceeded until the cry of the sleeper startled the midnight air – sealing her mouth with his palm, mastered by passion it was too late to desist and the rape was accomplished.

Neither spoke.

He left the room, ran down stairs, ran away by the corn cribs thinking she did not recognize him, and down to the river and secure darkness. He had not reached the granary and his couch before he heard the firing and the dogs barking. Why, it was certain he was unknown; if they knew it were he, such proceedings would not occur, so he thought.

The boys were tracking some unknown, no need or dogs or guns if Eugene were discovered as the culprit.

He breathed easier and felt secure.

Next day on some pretense or other he sent Dan down to Lunney's stable to spy their movements. After Lunney and Ellen left for the justice, he went away five miles to mow fox grass.

Here came to him Tom Lunney and John McKeniff saying: "Eugene, you better come with us to the river, there will be a warrant here in a short time anyway, so you just as well come now."

Such is their language as they and he told it, no dispute about this.

Now, were he innocent or ignorant of any crime in himself – his first question would be to his friends (and they did not speak to him then in any tone or anger). "What have you a warrant for me for?"

What, in fact did he say?

"Go to hell. Of course I'll not go with you without a warrant."

No guilt more palpably confessed.

After eating his dinner in a shed where all lingered, Eugene fell asleep on the hay on the floor while the two boys every now and then would kick his side telling him to come on down to the river.

This sleep would prove a disturbed slumber the night before.

After four hours of this waiting he never asked the charge against him.

At that time when constable Muzzy arrived and read the warrant, he said:

"And that's the reason those d—d sons of b——hs were hanging around here."

Innocence would not be so particular as to the legality of the arrest; were he innocent he would have learned the crime laid upon him, at least, and probably go without warrant.

Coward fear, trembling guilty possessed his heart and awed his senses.

Had he suspected a recognition his own fear would have driven him out of the country.

The preposterous alibi manufactured in his behalf has no defender.

In regard to the second opinion held, many people will not apologize for the killing when he was at his place for trial and ready to undergo the penalties of law. It would have been as well for all parties concerned to let the culprit live. However, not a few believe that the example set for rapists is worth the blood spilled and the money expended, so that purity be protected by exemplary vengeance, and secured by intimidation.

Coming to the third opinion; the verdict of the people, their acts and deeds make the law long before it finds its way in statutes. The civilized world has never executed a woman who avenges her wrongs, and while the cold letter of the law acts in bar to justification, common law (that practice which is in use to a time when the memory of man runs not to the contrary) arms the injured person and writes death on the clammy brow of the evil doer.

The third group of opinions is the one more liberally endorsed, and the one the jury after fair and impartial trial entertained. It seems to us to be a righteous verdict.

Few people give any credit phase of the question, although it deserves considerable attention; but, it takes experts on the conduct of the mind to draw the line between normal thought and derangement.

Let it pass – hoping that the girl's memory was, indeed, a blank; trusting that kindly nature threw over Miss Lunney's faculties at this awful, impassioned moment the subtle vesture of oblivion so that hereafter in the silences or at the hour of dissolution the agonized face of Eugene McEnroe may not look upon her for forgiveness or reproach, may not haunt her to distraction.

Haunt her to distraction it did, as the trial became a burden for the Lunney family to shoulder for years – even generations.

Most of the Lunneys stayed in Norton County, or adjoining Decatur County, and raised families. John and Anna Lunney spent the rest of their lives in Norton County, or nearby. The Irish in southwestern Norton County had been a close, clannish group with much intermarriage, and that continued. Two Lunney sisters married into the Costello family, an Irish family in the community that is pronounced, and often spelled, Costelloe. Mary married John Costello and Rose married Tom Costello, and they spent most of their lives in Norton or Decatur counties.

When he died December 4, 1917, at age eighty-one, John Lunney's obituary says he "possessed a ready wit and a genial nature" and he "made many friends."

"He had been in very poor health for a long time and had been a patient sufferer. He was active in the business affairs of his community," which indicates he was visible in the life of Lenora or New Almelo, or both.

Anna's obituary indicates the same. She had an active life out of the home and was not confined within its walls as was her daughter Ellen. Anna, or Ann as she often was called, died May 25, 1933,

Mary (Lunney) Costello in 1902 when she married Thomas Costello. Ellen wanted sister Mary to stay with her instead of accompanying her parents to visit Anna Lunney's sister, Sarah McKenna, and family in the summer of 1894. Had Mary stayed home, where she slept in the same bed as Ellen, the Lunney family's history might have avoided the rape and revenge that followed. (Photo courtesy of Caryl Finnerty, Fairfax, Va.)

at the home of her daughter, Rose, and her family. The obituary indicates she had lived with several of her children after her husband died.

Neither obituary mentioned the rape, murder or trial. Small town, local newspapers generally are gracious about leaving closet doors closed.

As John and Anna grew older, Thomas, the eldest son, became the manager of the Lunney farm and responsible for the care of the younger children. Tom purchased land of his own, regularly bought and sold cattle and was known as having a keen eye for judging livestock. He bought, fed and shipped cattle with Seywood Lar-

John Lunney in his later years with a child, probably one of his grandchildren. The patriarch of the family, Lunney arrived in America from Ireland as a young man and became one of the earliest homesteaders southwest of Lenora. Born in County Fermanagh, John left a sister, Catherine, in Ireland. He later brought Catherine's two sons, Hugh and John McKeniff, to live in Norton County. (Photo courtesy of Caryl Finnerty, Fairfax, Va.)

rick, the prominent Lenora banker who later gave the town a city park that still bears his name, and Austin Conkey of Edmond, who had become a family friend and business associate.

Tom seems to have been one of the victims of the depression of the 1930s. During the decade Tom sold much of his land holdings and, about the beginning of World War II, he moved to Denver where he died February 24, 1950.

Thomas never married.

Will Lunney, the second oldest son of John and Anna, lived his life in Lenora where he worked as a hired man. During years when alcohol could not be sold in Norton County, Will served as one of the town's most successful bootleggers. Will also never married.

His younger brother John (Jack) married, a union that produced a son. Jack Lunney became a prominent member of the Norton community who sustained his lifestyle mostly by gambling. He prided himself in his profession, always driving a new automobile and dressing as well as any man in Norton County. He also prided himself on not working at a routine job.

~

Ellen left the community for a while. In what probably was the first time she had ventured far from home, she went to Chicago to stay with an uncle and, according to family lore, worked for a woman of some wealth. It was there in the late 1890s that she met John Dwyer, a young Irishman who had come to this country in 1890 from Carrigaholt, a small community at the mouth of the River Shannon, in County Clare. As they say on the west coast of Ireland, the next parish to the west is Boston. The riverside along the Shannon where John O'Dwyer lived as a youth is not much more than a pile of rocks today. He lived so close to the river that the angry Shannon frequently threw rocks on the nearby O'Dwyer property. Finally, in the interest of their safety, the family moved the home a few feet up the riverbank from the river.

John O'Dwyer, the eldest of two sons, should have been at the front of the line to inherit the O'Dwyer family farm, but his parents wanted him to become a priest. John, who did not have the calling, disagreed. Instead he became a hedgerow teacher, helping young Irish children to learn reading and writing behind the hedgerows that separate the property in western Ireland. The English prohibited the Irish children from learning to read and write, and it was teachers like John who kept the Irish culture alive and strong. After it became apparent that his parents wanted younger brother Willie eventually to receive the farm, John left for America about 1890. On the trip the "O" fell off his name, and he became John Dwyer. He came to Chicago where he worked for the railroad for several years, saving money in hope of someday buying a farm. It was there that John met young Ellen Lunney.

Oral family history has it that Ellen and John came from Chicago to visit her parents with plans to marry in St. Joseph's Catholic

214

Church in New Almelo. However, the priest at the church refused to marry the young couple, apparently because of reasons relating to the the rape, murder and trial. The tumultuous trial obviously still was on the minds of those in southwestern Norton County. According to oral family history, John Dwyer had been unaware of the events of 1894 until he stood imbibing in a saloon in Lenora where a drinking companion told him about Ellen's history. John, shaken by the revelation, supposedly said he was taking the next train back to Chicago until the Lunney family persuaded him that marriage to Ellen meant a dowry of farmland. He reconsidered and returned with Ellen to Chicago where they were married November 28, 1898. They returned to live in a sod house they built on their new farm seven miles west of New Almelo in Decatur County, and the young couple quickly started a family. They raised six children: John, Nora, Ray, Wilma, Alice and Carl. About 1930 the family moved into a house at the edge of Lenora where John had sufficient space to raise pigs and cattle. He continued farming on land he had purchased or acreage that had been in the Lunney family. Except for son John, the first-born of the six children, none of the other children pursued a life on the farm.

Was John Dwyer a good catch for Ellen Lunney? The Lunneys seemed to think he was an excellent find. He was young and healthy with a basic education. The Lunneys must have known that the O'Dwyer clan, or sept, had been a significant family in Ireland, at least until Cromwell uprooted many of the old families like the O'Dwyers in the mid-seventeenth century. Historians have tracked the O'Dwyers to the barony of Kilnamanagh in the heartland of County Tipperary. The O'Dwyer's barony extended over an area of about one hundred square miles. The O'Dwyers were free clansmen under their tribal chief. Kilnamanagh means the "chapel of the monk" or the "wood of the monks." One poetic rendition refers to "the O'Dwyers of the fair teeth." The barony was between the town of Thurles and County Limerick.

Although the O'Dwyers were not one of the most powerful Irish clans, the family intermarried into some of the region's strongest families, the Butlers or Ormonds, the de Burgos or Bourkes, the Desmonds, O'Kennedys, O'Carrolls and MacCarthys. This resulted in a fierce bunch of O'Dwyers who spent decades resisting and fighting the English, even after Cromwell seized most of the O'Dwyer lands and scattered the survivors into less-settled areas of the west, especially counties Limerick and Clare.

The name of John O'Dwyer had considerable recognition through Ireland. Several persons by that name, or Dwyre, played prominent roles in Kilnamanagh and Dundrum. One male, part of the flight of "Wild Geese" from Ireland's shores to Europe, founded the French family of Haudoire. And an old Irish song pays tribute to a heroic defender named John O'Dwyer.

~

One other player in the Norton County drama of 1894, John McKeniff, would drift away from the rural countryside. The 1910 federal census finds McKeniff living in Kansas City, Kansas, and wed to a lady named Catherine, the name of his mother. Of Irish extraction, she came from New York state. The McKeniffs were raising a son, Harry, age six.

John McKeniff may have been infatuated by Ellen Lunney, and an unanswered question is how she responded. Ellen testified that she considered McKeniff as an older brother. A tall young Irish man with attractive looks may have held more than brotherly status, as the prosecution contended in arguments, but nothing ever was proven. Tom Lunney seemed to defer to the older McKeniff much as an older brother.

But it seemed time for McKeniff to seek his future elsewhere. In 1910 the census said he was employed in a Kansas City saloon. At one point McKeniff manged a liquor distributing company in Kansas City, Missouri. By 1920 the McKeniffs had a second child, Mary, age six. By then McKeniff was employed as a watchman in one of the meat-packing houses in Kansas City, Kansas.

~

Ellen never recovered from the shock of the events of 1894. When she told the jury she was ruined and degraded by the rape and wished Eugene McEnroe had killed her, Ellen seems to have been telling the complete truth. She valued her chastity so much that its loss without her consent meant she had been defiled and the purity of her womanhood had been stolen from her.

Nineteenth-century culture taught that a woman must guard her treasured virginity with her life. Ellen retaliated with the fury of a woman who had lost her main virtue, something she could never regain. She journeyed to Chicago to find what she could not on the plains, a husband who did not know her history.

Did she act alone or did the entire family conspire to help kill Eugene McEnroe? The trial never produced answers to those questions.

In the week after her rape, Ellen said she considered suicide. That may be the real reason the Norton County jury found her not guilty. The men on the jury understood the value she placed on her virtue and the loss of her chastity. She would kill for it, and the jury understood self defense. The jury must have looked for an excuse for killing Eugene McEnroe and found it easier to find her not guilty than to send her to prison. The jury also most likely understood the madness that Lafe Thompson and Clinton Angevine so tactfully brought into discussion in the trial. In the two weeks of the trial, those two attorneys clearly stood a head taller than the overworked prosecutors who tried to send Ellen to the penitentiary for a long period of time.

Later in life, after her children were grown, Ellen – known by this time as Ella – had become a virtual recluse, never straying far from her own home and never developing a group of friends outside her own family. Ella, by this time living in Lenora, left the home occasionally to shop in the town's businesses but she and her husband had little active social life. Ella regularly attended Sunday mass in New Almelo and kept a close relationship with her relatives, visiting them on Sunday and awaiting their calls to her home. John, apparently angered by the priest who refused to marry Ella and him, declined to participate in the church or any of its activities. Except for nearby neighbors, Ella rarely communicated with other families in the Protestant town of Lenora.

Ella retreated to the safety of the home and family, never knowing whether anyone with whom she might come in contact could have heard or read about the sensational trial in Norton years ago. She practically became a shut-in, although she was in good health until a stroke in 1957.

During the 1894 trial, a neighbor had described her as "backward," a judgment that seemed overly harsh. Part of her problem was that Ella never learned basic conversational skills to communicate with those whom she came in contact. She remained withdrawn and passive as though she awaited what else life might have in store for her.

The story of her rape surfaced in the 1930s when an enterprising reporter from a Norton newspaper decided the Lunney trial contained such a delicious story that it should be repeated. The story ran in one of the newspapers in the county seat.

Of course the story opened all the old wounds that had been trying for decades to heal. Ellen's youngest son, who knew nothing of his mother's rape and retaliation, was so amazed and in shock at what happened that he packed up and moved to California for about two years. When he returned, he had married and introduced his young bride to a startled family. Such was the shock of prying open and releasing the story of what happened on the High Plains in that one horrible week.

~

Ellen's husband, John Dwyer, died March 6, 1947. Before that time a divorced daughter, Nora Yocom, and her son Douglas, the author of this story, had moved into the Lenora home and lived with Ella. After Ella had a stroke in 1957, she became a semi-invalid and moved into the Andbe Home in Norton where she lived until her death in 1961. Most of the Dwyer children never told their children about the trial of Ellen, or Ella, by then the matriarch of the family. The rape, the killing and the trial never were discussed and, if a child heard a scrap of information about the events, they usually were told it was something not talked about by the family.

I grew to manhood in my grandparent's house, and I still don't know how they and the rest of the Lunneys and Dwyers kept the trial a secret from everyone. The family simply avoided discussing the rape and subsequent events, hoping the passage of time would erase the memories of those who knew what happened. Although I lived under my grandmother's roof, I first heard about the rape, murder and trial from a cousin in 2002. It stunned me. Eventually I made my way to what records were available to research and write the story.

Ella Dwyer died on March 30, 1961, and was buried beside her husband John Dwyer in St. Joseph's Cemetery in New Almelo – ironically less than one hundred yards from the grave of Eugene McEnroe, who is buried at the south end of the same cemetery.

No doubt the feelings and anger ran high for years in the Lunney household whenever the thought of Gene McEnroe entered the consciousness of a family member. But the burial of Ella in the same cemetery where Eugene McEnroe eternally rested tells something about how well the passage of time washes away the memory of the rape and trial. A walk through the cemeteries at New Almelo and Lenora will find the grave sites of many of the main characters in the drama of the sensational trial that riveted the attention of the citizens of Norton County in 1894.

If Ella's children knew about the events of 1894 and thought about them at her death or the death of her husband John Dwyer in 1947, nobody bothered to provide much separation between the graves of the two main characters in that drama. The clash in life seemed to resolve itself after the death of the parties, a reconciliation that never occurred until the quietness of death overtook them.

Sources

American Heritage. *American Manners and Morals, A Picture History of How We Behaved and Misbehaved.* American Heritage Book Division, 1969.

Bader, Robert Smith. *Prohibition in Kansas.* Lawrence, Kansas: University Press of Kansas, 1986.

Baker, Ray Stannard. *American Chronicle.* New York: Charles Scribner's Sons, 1945.

Bowers, D. N. *Seventy Years in Norton County, Kansas, 1872-1942.* Norton, Kansas: Norton County *Champion*, 1942.

Bright, John D. *Kansas, the First Century, Volume One.* New York: Lewis Historical Publishing Co., 1956.

Browne, Angela. *When Battered Women Kill.* New York: The Free Press, 1987.

Callanan, Martin. *Records of Four Tipperary Septs.* Galway: O'Gorman Ltd., Printinghouse, 1938.

Clanton, Gene. *Populism, The Humane Preference in America.* Boston: Twayne Publishers, 1989.

Clanton, O. Gene. *Kansas Populism, Ideas and Men.* Lawrence, Kansas: University Press of Kansas, 1969.

Columbian History of Education in Kansas. Compiled by Kansas Educators. Topeka: Hamilton Printing Company, 1893.

Dary, David A. *The Buffalo Book.* Swallow Press/Ohio University Press, 1989.

Dary, David A. *Cowboy Culture, A Saga of Five Centuries.* University Press of Kansas, 1989.

Dick, Everett. *The Sod-House Frontier, 1854-1890.* Lincoln, Nebraska: University of Nebraska Press, 1979.

Diggs, Annie L. *The Story of Jerry Simpson.* Wichita, Kansas: Hopson Printing Company and Jane Simpson, 1908.

Dieterich, Virgil C. *A Story of Lenora, Kansas, 1873-1974.* Privately printed, 1974.

Einsel, Mary. *The Priceless Prairie.* Privately printed, 1976.

Faragher, John Mack. *Rereading Frederick Jackson Turner, The Significance of the Frontier in American History and Other Essays.* New York City: Henry Holt, 1994.

Ford, Henry Jones. *The Cleveland Era, A Chronicle of the New Order in Politics.* New Haven, Connecticut: Yale University Press, 1920.

221

Fourteenth Biennial Report of the Kansas Board of Agriculture. Topeka, Kansas, 1905.

Gard, Wayne. *The Great Buffalo Hunt.* New York: Alfred A. Knopf, 1960.

Gerber, Rudolph Joseph. *The Insanity Defense.* Port Washington, New York: Associated Facility Press, 1984.

Ghent, W. J. *The Road to Oregon, A Chronicle of the Great Immigrant Trail.* New York: Longmans, Green and Co., 1929.

Gillespie, Cynthia. *Justifiable Homicide, Battered Women, Self-Defense and the Law.* Columbus, Ohio: Ohio State University Press, 1989.

Glaab, Charles N. *The American City, A Documentary History.* Homewood, Ill.: The Dorsey Press, 1963.

_____. *The Grand Duke Alexis in the United States of America.* New York: Interland Publishing, Inc., 1972 (originally printed as *His Imperial Highness The Grand Duke Alexis in the United States of America During the Winter of 1871-72.* For Private Distribution by the Riverside Press, Cambridge, 1972).

Greeley, Horace. *An Overland Journey, from New York to San Francisco in the Summer of 1859.* Lincoln: University of Nebraska Press, 1999.

Hickert, John W. *The First Eighty Years in New Almelo.* Norton, Kansas: Wilson Carter Printers, 1969.

Hicks, John D. *The Populist Revolt, A History of the Farmers' Alliance and the People's Party.* Lincoln, Nebraska: University of Nebraska Press, 1961.

Hutchinson, C. C. *Resources of Kansas, Fifteen Years Experience.* Topeka, Kansas: Published by the author, 1871.

Ise, John. *Sod and Stubble.* Lincoln, Nebraska: University of Nebraska Press, 1967.

Jauken, Arlene Feldmann. *The Moccasin Speaks, Living as Captives of the Dog Soldier Warriors, Red River War 1874-1875.* Lincoln, Nebraska: Dagforde Publishing, 1998.

Lass, William E. *From the Missouri to the Great Salt Lake, An Account of Overland Freighting.* Nebraska State Historical Society, 1972.

Lockard, Frank. *History of Norton County.* Kansas: Norton County *Champion*, 1894.

Lathrop, Amy. *Tales of Western Kansas.* Norton, Kansas, self-published, 1948.

McNall, Scott G. *The Road to Rebellion, Class Formation and Kansas Populism, 1865-1900.* Chicago: University of Chicago Press, 1988.

Miller, Nyle H., and Snell, Joseph W. *Why the West Was Wild.* Topeka: Kansas State Historical Society, 1963.

Miner, H. Craig, and Unrau, William E. *The End of Indian Kansas, A Study in Cultural Revolution, 1854-1871.* Lawrence, Kansas: The Regents Press of Kansas, 1978.

Miner, Craig. *West of Wichita, Settling the High Plains of Kansas, 1865-1890.* Lawrence, Kansas: The Regents Press of Kansas, 1986.

Myres, Sandra L. *Westering Women and the Frontier Experience.* Albuquerque: New Mexico Press, 1982.

Ninth Biennial Report of the Kansas State Board of Agriculture. Topeka, Kansas, 1895.

O'Dwyer, Sir Michael. *The O'Dwyers of Kilnamanagh, The History of An Irish Sept.* London: John Murray, 1933.

Peak, Kenneth J., and Patricia A. *Kansas Temperance, Much Ado About Booze, 1870-1920.* Manhattan, Kansas: Sunflower University Press, 2000.

Pickett, Calder M. *Ed Howe, Country Town Philosopher.* Lawrence: University Press of Kansas, 1968.

Reynolds, John N. *A Kansas Hell or Life in the Kansas Penitentiary.* Atchison, Kansas: The Bee Publishing Co., 1889.

Seale, William. *The President's House, a History.* Washington, D. C.: White House Historical Association, 1986.

Schlereth, Thomas J. *Victorian America, Transformations in Everyday Life.* New York: HarperCollins, 1991.

Schwantes, Carlos A. *Coxey's Army, An American Odyssey.* Lincoln, Nebraska: University of Nebraska Press, 1985.

Schwendemann, Glen. "Nicodemus: Negro Haven on the Solomon." *Kansas Historical Quarterly,* Spring, 1968, pp 10-31.

Sinks, Perry Wayland. *Popular Amusements and the Christian Life.* Chicago: Fleming H. Revell, 1896.

Smith, Anthony. *The Newspaper, An International History.* London: Thames and Hudson, 1979.

Stratton, Joanna L. *Pioneer Women, Voices From the Kansas Frontier.* New York: Simon and Schuster, 1981.

Speed, P. F. *The Potato Famine and the Irish Emigrants.* Essex, England: Longman House, 1983.

Train, Arthur. *Courts and Criminals.* New York: Charles Scribner's Sons, 1926.

Tugwell, Rexford Guy. *Grover Cleveland.* New York: The Macmillan Company, 1968.

Unruh, John D. *The Plains Across, The Overland Emigrants and the Trans-Mississippi West, 1840-60.* Urbana and Chicago: University of Illinois Press, 1979.

Vestal, Stanley. *Queen of the Cowtowns, Dodge City.* Lincoln, Nebraska: Bison, University of Nebraska Press, 1972.

Webb, Walter Prescott. *The Great Plains.* New York: Grosset & Dunlap, 1931.

Winther, Oscar Osburn. *The Transportation Frontier, Trans-Mississippi West, 1865-1890.* Albuquerque, New Mexico: University of New Mexico Press, 1964.

Woodward, C. Vann. *Tom Watson, Agrarian Rebel.* New York: Oxford University Press, 1963.

Zornow, William Frank. *Kansas, a History of the Jayhawk State.* Norman, Oklahoma: University of Oklahoma Press, 1957.

Newspapers

Lenora News. Lenora, Kansas, February 4, 1909.
Lenora Record. Lenora, Kansas, September 2, 1887, to February 20, 1890.
Lenora Times. Lenora Kansas, February 4, 1893, to June 3, 1893.
Lenora Sun. Lenora, Kansas, March 6, 1890, to June 26, 1890.
The Liberator. Norton Kansas, August 18, 1893, to May 26, 1896.
Norton Champion. Norton, Kansas, May 1, 1894, to December 30, 1894.
Norton Courier. Norton, Kansas, May 1, 1894, to December 30, 1894.